GET YOUR BOOK INTO AUSTRALIAN LIBRARIES

Sell more books, earn more royalties

EBONY MCKENNA

Ebony McKenna Publishing

Copyright © 2018 by Ebony McKenna

All rights reserved.

ISBN: 978-0-6482842-0-8

Cover design by Lana Pecherczyk

No part of this book may be reproduced in any form or by any electronic or mechanical means, including information storage and retrieval systems, without written permission from the author, except for the use of brief quotations in a book review.

All care has been taken (oops, passive voice) to make sure this book is accurate at the time of publication.

For the hard-working librarians across Australia

CONTENTS

Introduction — vii

PART ONE
1. Selling more books, earning more royalties — 3
2. ISBN au-go-go — 9
3. Becoming your own publisher — 14
4. Assigning ISBNs to each title — 19
5. The cost of print runs — 26
6. Pricing your books — 30

PART TWO
7. Getting ready to earn royalties — 39
8. Judging a book by its cover — 41
9. Registering for Lending Rights — 45
10. Deadlines for Lending Rights — 53
11. Australias big library suppliers — 55
12. Contacting library suppliers — 59
13. Invoices — 61

PART THREE
14. Sell sheets — 67
15. Creating library lists — 74
16. Contacting libraries — 91
17. Bringing it all together — 96
18. School suppliers — 98
19. One More Thing — 102
20. MARC records — 103

Also by Ebony McKenna   106
Acknowledgments   107

INTRODUCTION

This book started life as a four-week online workshop with the Romance Writers of Australia (RWA) and then it became an ebook, packed with links that took you to exactly the pages you'd need.

Now it's a paperback.

Links don't work so well in paper, but that's OK, we'll still get plenty done, and have plenty to show for it.

This book is a guide for authors to get their books into libraries across Australia. It will help authors sell more books and earn more royalties, in initial sales and further down the track with Lending Rights.

It will also be a handy go-to for librarians, to hand over to well-meaning local authors who turn up to donate their books.

WHO IS THIS?

I'm your host with the mos–ADHD, Ebony McKenna. I'm the author of 7 YA romance novels, loads of short stories, and anthologies. I'm also the author of two 'Edit Your Own' guides

INTRODUCTION

for writers: *Edit Your Own Romance Novel* and *Edit Your Own YA Novel*. All of these books, except for the short stories, are in libraries across Australia. Everything I did to get those books on the shelves is compiled in this book. The one you're reading in paperback, which I bet you picked up in a library.

The fact you're reading this in a library shows you that the system works. It works for me, it can work for you too.

I've made plenty of mistakes and wasted loads of time in the past few years. That's human nature. Now I've climbed out of the pits I fell in, I've mapped out a more direct course, so you can learn from my mistakes.

I will stress up front, this book covers a fair amount of territory. It's a good way to get your books into libraries, but it's not the ONLY way to do it. The landscape is in a state of flux and things change rapidly. But it is an efficient, professional way to get your books into libraries where the author legitimately sells books, which the libraries want, and readers will read.

This book will primarily work for self-published authors as well as authors published with small presses. Traditionally published authors will also learn plenty about the process and will be able to give their books a nudge in the right direction if they need to.

This book will also work for everyone who wants to earn 'Lending Rights' with their printed books. Even those of us published with 'big name' publishers can sometimes miss out on Lending Rights, because the editors or publishers assumed we knew about them already.

Lending Rights are PLR and ELR; Public Lending Rights and Educational Lending Rights. This is a payment for the number of copies of your books on public and school library shelves. (Not the number of times they are borrowed). You get the payment once a year and it really is fabulous.

Lending Rights are not available for ebooks in Australia – yet. BUT readers borrow plenty of ebooks (through Overdrive and many others) from libraries, so this is a great opportunity to get your books in front of readers' eyeballs. It's also an excellent time to join the Australian Society of Authors, who are the reason we have Lending Rights at all, and are actively campaigning for Digital Lending Rights at the moment.

GET THE TIMING RIGHT!

Generally, public libraries' budgeted years run from January to December. They have money to spend on books earlier in the year. It's often the same for school libraries too.

Or, when it's getting closer to the end of their financial year, they can sometimes have money 'left over' in the budget, which they need to spend before the year runs out.

Many are on a July to June financial year like the rest of us tax-paying schlubs, which is incredibly helpful as that means lots of purchases in March and November for one lot, and many more in June and August for others. (I had a lovely order of 28 books from one library service in mid-June last year. Happy EOFY to me!)

It's all about getting your figurative ducks in a row, so that when the time comes for you to contact libraries and show them your brilliant book/s, everything will be in place for the library to place orders from official channels without any hassles.

Your book will be wanted by the library, paid for in fact, it will be in the catalogue and be available for borrowing from the public.

I can't stress enough how important it is to do things in the right order.

In fact, it's why I wrote this book.

PART ONE

Doing things in the right order, right from the start.

Chapter One

SELLING MORE BOOKS, EARNING MORE ROYALTIES

Because that's what we're here for

I can't tell you the number of authors I've met over the years who tell me the way to get a book into a library is to turn up to the local branch and donate them.

Even when I've explained this isn't a good idea (and it's not a sustainable business model) they then look for some wriggle room and ask, 'what if I make an appointment?' and then I sigh.

Are you writing books plural? Are you keen to make a real career out of this and be compensated for your artistic toil?

If yes, then keep right on reading.

It bears repeating that this book is a demonstration of my self-publishing business model. This book you are holding in your hands is a book that libraries have officially paid for and want to have in their collections. (Which is rather thrilling, and good for the ego.) It's part of my business plan to have this and other titles in libraries - for the initial sales and, later down the track, royalties from Lending Rights. It's a far more reliable business model than trying to sell into book stores, with short shelf-lives and high risks of returns.

Before we go any further. On behalf of librarians and

resource & collections managers everywhere, please don't donate your books.

Why? You ask innocently enough.

1. You look unprofessional
2. Did they even know you were coming?
3. Where will they catalogue the books if they didn't know you were coming?
4. Awkwards!
5. Most importantly, if your book does prove popular, how is the library going to order more copies in? Will they call you to donate more? Donating books is not a sustainable business model.
6. This is the business side of writing, treat it as a business.
7. Librarians are incredibly busy. Yes, even if an author 'makes an appointment with the chief librarian'. (There's no such thing as a 'Chief Librarian'. They're Collection Managers or Resource Managers, so if you request an appointment with the 'Chief Librarian' they'll already know you're not keeping up.)
8. Lending Rights are calculated on the number of titles on the shelves across the country, not the number of times a book is borrowed. It's true that having one copy of your book in a mobile library does make it available for people 'all over' to borrow, it's only one copy. And you dontated that. Which isn't a stable business model. We're all about making a stable buisness model.

GET YOUR BOOK INTO AUSTRALIAN LIBRARIES

Here's what you will do instead of donating your book/s to your local library:

1. **Buy Australian ISBNs** from Thorpe Bowker / myidentifiers.com.au
2. **Assign an ISBN** to each of your book titles, and each format. Ie, one ISBN for paperback, one for hardcover (if you're doing hardcover) and one for ebooks.
3. **Publish your ebook** to the world, if you're publishing electronically.
4. **Publish your print book** to the world if you're going into print, which I highly recommend. This will involve several stages of choosing a printer and selecting distribution. Ingram Spark are my personal favourite, and they now list major library suppliers amongst their distribution channels, meaning the suppliers can order directly from the printer, saving you the author time and money in postage and handling.
5. Work out your **pricing**, especially for print editions. Pricing includes **postage costs** – where you might only break even or lose some money up front to get your books into libraries, but you'll make it back with PLR and then some. You'll also need to work out **discounts** for library suppliers (some of them want such deep discounts you'll wonder if it's worth it.)
6. Contact **official library suppliers** around Australia – I'll provide a list for you to contact individually, as professionally as possible. This will involve filling out multiple forms for some, and sending emails to others. As you will have all your information in your 'myidentifyers' page on Thorpe Bowker, you can copy

5

and paste the information each time, instead of writing it out over and over.
7. Make '**sell sheets**' which you can email out to libraries.
8. Contact the **actual libraries** themselves to let them know your books are listed with official library suppliers, and send them your sell sheets. (See how far down this is on the list? It's basically your second last stage. That's why you don't just print your books and donate them to the library yourself.)
9. Register for **Lending Rights** – step-by-step instructions for how to fill out the forms and get future royalties every year for your printed books! Yes, our taxes at work!

That's a lot to get through!
Luckily, I've broken tasks into manageable chunks so we can check things off as we go.

SIDE NOTE: Before I self-published, I was traditionally published and my books 'magically' turned up in libraries.
I really had no idea how this happened, but I very much enjoyed receiving Lending Rights.
On one hand my books 'weren't selling' (or in reality, not selling enough) yet they were on library shelves AND STAYING THERE. Libraries have thousands of books vying for shelf space and somehow my first two Ondine novels held their own.
That showed me they were being borrowed regularly. If not, they would have been shunted aside for books that were more popular.

YOUR FIRST SET OF TASKS:

It's time to get to work already. In order to get ready, you need to prepare your book/s for sale to library suppliers:

- Buy your ISBNs from the Australia's official ISBN retailer, Thorpe Bowker Australia (www.myidentifiers.com.au)
- Assign one ISBN to each format of your book (if you're creating ebooks, paperbacks and hardbacks for example).
- Make yourself (or your writing name) the publisher if you're self-publishing.
- Work out book prices **for your print runs or print on demand costs**.

Writers published with small and large presses, you are definitely part of this too.

You won't need to do quite as much work as self-published authors. Your publishers will have assigned an ISBN to your book and they are the ones who pay for the print runs.*

But you will need to create an information file for each of your titles, because you will need this information when you contact official library suppliers.

There is a lot to take in and it can be confusing at first, but you'll get there. Please keep reading through all the stages - even if they don't specifically apply to you right now. It's handy to know, and if you're looking at self-publsihing, you'll know exactly what to do.

* Why is there an asterisk? It's because if you truly are published, (whether small press or large) it's your publisher who

pays for the print runs. That's the whole deal about *being published*. They are the ones taking the risk because they think they can make money from your book.

If the author is the one paying for the printing, or sharing the costs of printing, or in any way sending money to the publisher, then I'm afraid the author is involved in what's called 'subsidy publishing' or 'vanity publishing'. That means you are not the publisher. They may have provided an ISBN (big whoop!) but in all honesty, vanity publishers pretty much take on anyone who can pay. It's not about literary merit, it's about earning money from authors (as opposed to earling money by selling books to readers and libraries, which is how it really works.) If you find yourself in one of these situations, get out while you still can. You may as well self-publish - it's cheaper and more credible.

Chapter Two

ISBN AU-GO-GO

(and don't stress about bar codes)

Every physical book needs an ISBN (International Standard (or Standardised) Book Number) in order to:

1. Help libraries and library suppliers order the right book
2. Claim Lending Rights further down the track for the author.
3. Claim Lending Rights further down the track for the publisher - which may also be you. That's right, you get publisher royalties as well.

Even if you're only publishing ebooks at the moment, you still need to know how this works. (And then, honestly, what are you waiting for? Get into print!)

If your ebooks are already published on Kindle with an amazon ASIN (Amazon's version of the ISBN), that's fine for now, but if you want your ebooks in libraries and you want to make sure you are listed as the publisher (instead of Kindle or Blurb or Smashwords being your 'publisher',) then consider buying and using your own ISBNs to create editions that are truly yours.

This means when Digital Lending Rights come in - and the campaign is underway - you will get payments for book copies as the author and publisher.

Being the publisher means buying ISBNs and registering them as 'yours' in YOUR NAME, or a publishing name that you create.

Some internet organisations will sell you 100 ISBNs for $10 - which seems amazing up front. However, after you buy them you realise the ISBNs can't have you listed as the publisher but some mob called 'ISBNFactoryThanksForYourMoney' etc. You've just blown $10, but worse than that, you've wasted your time.

Some printers and distributors offer ISBNs as well, like CreateSpace (CS) and IngramSpark (IS) but beware you don't lock yourself out of potential markets by doing this. Here's some interesting information from www.self-publishingadvice.com:

> ISBNs
>
> CS offers several options for ISBNs. The free and $10 options are only good if you only want to distribute solely through CS; they can't be used anywhere else. The $99 option can be used elsewhere, but *not* if you opt into expanded distribution. Here's why.
>
> As we already discussed, CS uses Ingram for distribution. So if you purchase the CS ISBN *and* opt for expanded distribution, when you go to publish with Ingram and use the same

ISBN, it will show as already being in their system, as CS has it assigned.

There are two ways around this.

Buy the CS ISBN for $99 but *do not* opt into the expanded distribution.

Buy an ISBN from Ingram Spark (less money) and use that for both Ingram and CS.

Of course the other option is to use your own ISBN, which is my preferred choice.

Visit the www.self-publishingadvice.com website for plenty of up-to-date information about the industry. Keep in mind this is a US site and may not cater to Australian needs.

I recommend Australian authors buy their ISBNs from Thorpe Bowker (TB) in Australia. TB are the official retailer of ISBNs in this country, and you will be registered as the publisher., either under your own name or a publishing name you create. I know I'm repeating myself, but that's because it's important.

YOUR FIRST JOB (HOW EXCITING!)

Type the link below into your laptop/computer and follow the instructions to register with **myidentifiers**, so that you're ready to purchase your ISBNs. https://www.myidentifiers.com.au

You'll see some prices on offer. It might make your stomach do that hideous swooping thing.

1 ISBN for $44? That's a bit steep.

10 ISBNs though is 'only' $88 and makes much more sense.

100 ISBNs is $480, an excellent bulk deal, and perfect for writers with several books in a few formats each.

BAR CODES

I don't bother buying bar codes for two reasons.

1. I can find bar code creator bots on the web, just by doing a search.
2. Ingram Spark and other printers automatically create a bar code (based on your ISBN) and position it on the back cover when you use their free cover template creators.

THE OUCHY BIT.

The first time you buy from My Identifiers/Thorpe Bowker, they'll hit you with a $55 'set up' fee. (As of July 2018) It still works out at a good price per ISBN, and it's only when you first buy your ISBNs. Buying from Thorpe Bowker means you're purchasing official ISBNs *and* you'll be **recording the details in a recognised database**, which will help you later on when you register for Lending Rights. Your ISBN must be in a recognised database for it to be registered for Lending Rights. Thorpe Bowker/myidentifiers is that database.

Once you get your ISBNs, remember this:

You can only use each ISBN once. Once you've used it, you can't then cancel the book you've assigned it to and re-use the ISBN for a new book. That means take your time and try not to make (expensive) mistakes.

As I said earlier, each format of your book needs its own ISBN. For example, a paperback edition in 5x8 size needs a different ISBN to a 6x9 'large print' edition. If you are keen to make a hardcover, or hardback edition, you'll need an ISBN for that as well.

You'll need a different ISBN for an ebook too. BUT you can

format a single ebook with one ISBN and that book then becomes the kobo, kindle, ibook edition etc. This is because you're the publisher and you're making the ebook. It will be the same 'edition' with the same cover, so it only needs one ISBN. This will be handy when you're registering your book with Overdrive so your ebook can go out to libraries - one ISBN per title makes it easier for them and you.

HONESTY TIME:

I have seven novels out, in paperback, in libraries. (#Humblebrag) and a few reference non-fiction titles. So far, I haven't really bothered with promoting the ebooks to libraries. I write Young Adult, and research shows most teens love holding physical books. I keep reading research that explains iPads make teens feel like they're doing homework, as most of them use iPads for school stuff.

However, adults also read YA, so I need to get my ebooks out there into libraries. Which means I'll be following all my own advice as we go along. I'm on this journey with you. (Which also means I'll need to buy some more ISBNs!)

Further down the track, when you come to register with Public Lending Right, you must match your ISBNs to each paperback. Frustratingly, PLR is only for physical books at this stage and not ebooks, but I'm campaigning for this to change.

Has your stomach done another flip because you don't have paperbacks? That's OK. It's important to get your ebooks into libraries – it's where the readers are, and you want readers. I hope that as you work through this guide book, you'll see that although going into print is daunting, it's achievable.

If I can do it with my squirrel brain, then you can too.

Chapter Three

BECOMING YOUR OWN PUBLISHER

Because you're in business now, so treat this as a business

You're buying your own ISBNs, which officially makes you the publisher of your books.

That means when you put your ebooks and print books out there for sale, you use the ISBN registered to you. Please remember to use your author name or your publishing house/company name.

You don't have to start a whole new company. Just use your author name. Or something. You can register a business name if you want (with the ATO) and get yourself an ABN and be in acronym heaven. Knock yourself out.

I made a dopey mistake when I put an earlier book through Ingram Spark and selected my married name as the publisher. Whoops! That's my legal name but not my author name. (My author name is still technically my legal name, but still.) Not a huge problem, and I've fixed it now. It's not like writing Young Adult is going to get me fired from my workplace. (Because I work from home.) But if you work for - just spitballing here - a conservative religious organisation, or you're planning a tilt at politics, it might be a good idea to have the publisher / author name separate from the surname people know and love you for, and not something that might land you in trouble.

PUTTING YOUR BOOKS OUT THERE.

This is obviously a very important stage. I assume most authors are fairly familiar with the process of creating ebooks and print books, whether as a print run or POD (print on demand) or putting things through Smashwords/Draft2Digital/Amazon etc.

Rather than re-invent that wheel, here's a brilliant website to check out, looking at the pros and cons of Ingram Spark and Create Space for your print books. Sorry for the long link, but type this into a new browser and have a read.

https://selfpublishingadvice.org/watchdog-ingram-spark-vs-createspace-for-self-publishing-print-books/

Something else to remember. Ingram Spark prints in Australia. Create Space does not. That means the shipping costs will probably be higher if you're ordering print runs from the USA.

BONUS

I have put this bonus further in the book so that people who have read this far get the benefit - rather than just people flicking through the first few pages.

I have not had to pay to list any of my paperbacks with Ingram Spark. (But I have ordered plenty of books, so they've made money from me, no problem!)

How did I get this freebie?

By paying attention whenever I'm on the 'checkout' page of any internet website. There's usually a section that asks for a discount coupon. But I don't have one to hand - which is OK. All I do is open a new browser window and search 'Company name, discount coupon', then I scroll through the results.

I try a few coupons, and see which ones work.

Every time I've found a discount coupon for Ingram Spark, it has worked and the fee has gone from US $49 to $0. That's a pretty great success rate, yeah?

So if you bought this book, it's just paid for itself and then some. They are out there and they are easy to find.

* * *

When I publish ebooks, I format them using Vellum software and then use Draft2Digital (D2D) to distribute the .epub file to just about every retail store.

You can also use D2D to format your ebooks for free, and they have some handy templates for story genres.

Prior to D2D I used Smashwords. It was basic and easy to follow. However, I struck trouble when I tried to load an anthology with multiple authors. Smashwords wouldn't list the title unless I listed every contributing author as a 'Smashwords author'. It was honestly too much effort, so I went over to D2D.

Even though Draft2Digital will load directly to Amazon, by doing so they take too much of a royalty, so I load my Kindle edition ebooks directly on to Amazon, using KDP (Kindle Direct Publishing) to load up the .mobi formatted file into their system.

Draft2digital allows you to select 'Overdrive' the company that supplies ebooks to libraries across Australia and the world. Select Overdrive when you're publishing an ebook and you're all set to get your ebooks into libraries.

WARNING: Overdrive won't show up as a distribution option unless your book price is $1.99 or above. I don't know why.

For print, I use Ingram Spark. I had previously used Blurb, but I.S. is more appealing to local bookstores who may want to order my titles directly.

Blurb are user friendly, and they print in the same place as Ingram Spark (in Scoresby, Victoria). The quality is very good, and the binding is sturdy, which appeals to libraries. Choose 'gloss' cover as this is more durable than 'matte'.

Blurb is excellent if you have novels with footnotes (cough) or want to do extra clever things with formatting and shapes within your book. However, once you're done, you will sit at your desk for up to 45 minutes as it 'uploads' to the printer. People are complaining about slow NBN download speeds, but the *upload* speeds have always been deliberately throttled at 2 Mbps. Which is a rant for another day, an hoo boy, do I get ranty about that!

You can use CreateSpace via Amazon for print editions, and I have used them in the past. The printing is excellent. However, as I mentioned earlier, CreateSpace print in the USA, so the postage killed me getting the books delivered to my home in Victoria. Then again, friends in Western Australia found Create Space to be cheaper with shipping, so choose what's best for you.

I've also heard great things about using Fuji Xerox (in Tassie) for print runs. You can do all sorts of fabulous things with the covers, so please check them out.

I'm a little wary of Lulu, because the few copies I've seen from them have thick white paper (ideal for photos and non-fiction, not so great for novels). This could be down to the author's choices, I'm not sure. Also, the cost per book with Lulu gets pretty steep, whereas the copies I make from Ingram Spark are around the $6.50 mark for a 250 – 300 page paperback novel in 5x8). On the plus side, Lulu will let you pick up your print order and save on postage. Ingram Spark will let you pick the books up from the factory, but they still charge you for the shipping anyway.

I'm going to let you investigate the best way for you to format your ebooks and print books. (And I haven't even mentioned cover art!) Google freely and read widely to learn all you can. It's a whole other workshop in itself, really. (Why yes, I am running self-publishing workshops, thanks for asking!)

Chapter Four

ASSIGNING ISBNS TO EACH TITLE

(and each format of each title, if you have hardcovers and paperbacks of the same book)

This bit is fun. I've taken heaps of screen grabs, to give you a general idea of what page you should be on. Please don't stress if you can't read all the detail in the photos - the point of the exercise is to give you guidelines. First place to visit is www.myidentifiers.com for Thorpe Bowker Indentifier Services.

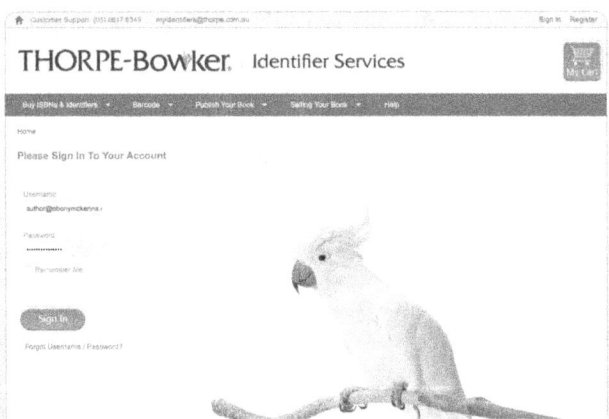

Now you're ready to assign an ISBN to your first title, and, by extension, using your author name as your publisher (or coming up with a publishing house name if you want to go there.)

This is a time-intensive procedure, **please slow down and take your time**. You will spend half an hour filling out a form on the internet, which relies on decent download and upload speeds. I hope you have good network connection and patience aplenty. I'll take you through the process. Grab a cuppa and a snack.

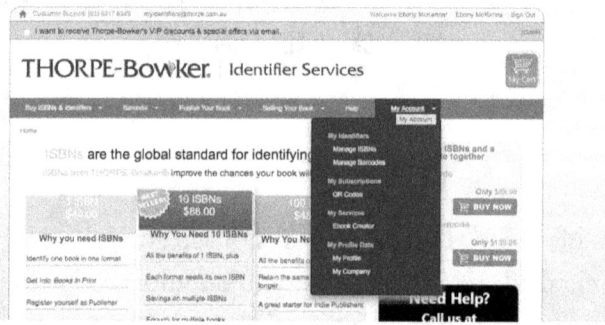

Welcome to the Myidentifiers / Thorpe Bowker front page. Sign yourself in. In the previous image, you can see I've signed in with my author email address and my top-secret password. (Which you created back when you bought the ISBNs.) Once you sign in, select 'My Account' from that menu bar under the Thorpe Bowker logo in the next picture. This creates a drop-down menu.

Select 'My Identifiers' at the top of those choices.

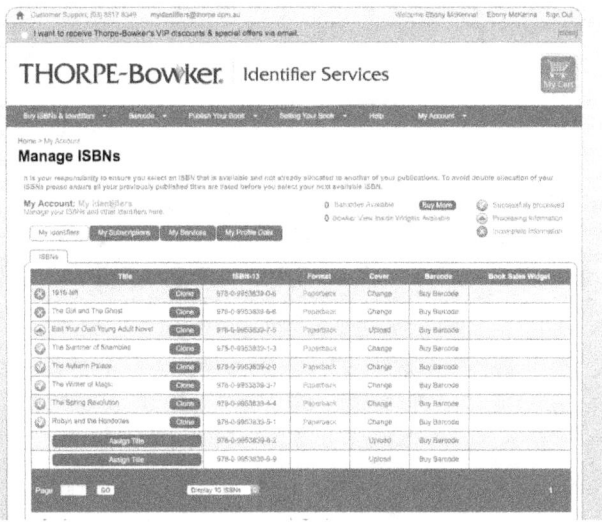

The above picture shows the 10 ISBNs I own. I've filled nearly all of them in. When you've filled them in correctly and completely, you'll get a green market next to the book title. Yellow is 'processing' and red means incomplete.

There's an ISBN for each title – as they are all paperbacks at this point. I haven't made hardbacks, nor have I made large print.

The excellent thing about ISBNs is that they're international. So each paperback title only needs one ISBN for the whole world. (When you sell through printers like Blurb and Ingram Spark, they make print editions available through web-based bookstores worldwide.)

OK, let's get look at how we assign an ISBN to a book.

For this demonstration, I clicked on the second title - *The Girl and The Ghost*. It's very hard to read the text in the image, so trust me on this.

I've filled in some but not all the details. You don't have to fill in every single detail, just the most important ones with the red asterisks. (However, the more information you do give, the more information library suppliers will have.)

When you start doing the same thing for one of your titles, you'll notice the essential sections of each title listing has a red asterisk. Everything else is something you can fill in later if you want to.

GLITCH AHEAD

If you copy and paste your book's description/blurb from a word file into the "Main Description" section on this website form, you'll need to read over it and put in spaces after full stops at the paragraph returns. I'm not sure why the spaces sometimes vanish in a copy and paste, they just do.

If there's something you're not sure of, click on the grey question mark next to each section for an explanation.

After each page, click on the 'save' button to save the details, then click onto the next section and fill that out.

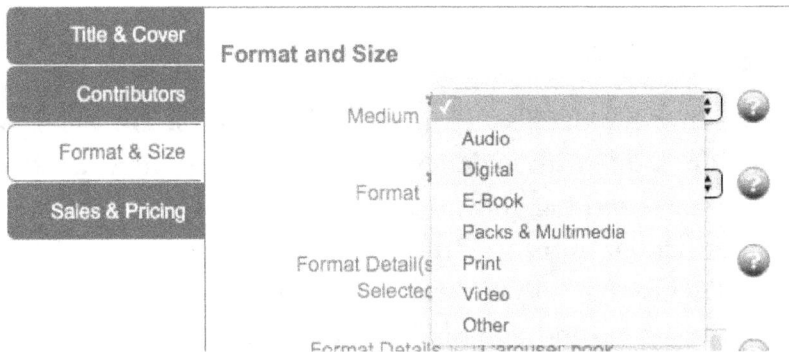

As my example is for a paperback, I've selected paperback on the 'Format and Size' page. If you're assigning an ISBN to an ebook, you'll need to select ebook.

When you're finished, make sure you click the 'submit' button on the bottom of the 'Sales and Pricing' page.

When you go back to the screen listing your ISBNs you'll get a yellow marker next to the title, showing that the title is now being processed.

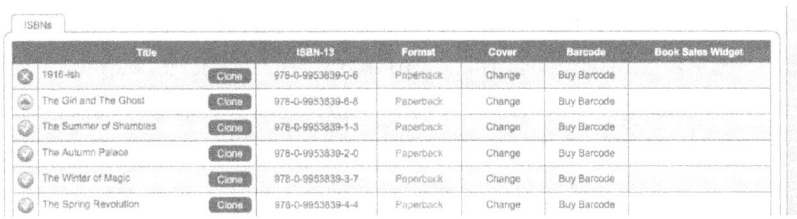

How cool was that? You just assigned your first (of many!) ISBNs.

The reason you fill all these details in at this point is because bookstore 'bots' on the internet search for details of your title to display on their websites. These bots can grab all the information about your book titles from the POD printers as well, but it's good to have things registered and official.

POTENTIAL GLITCHES!

Make sure the details in your ISBN allocation are as consistent as possible with whichever printer service you're using.

If you're writing romantic time travel, then make sure the words 'fiction, romance, time travel' appear in the category details with your printer and with your ISBN allocation, and with every retail and publishing outlet. In other words, **get these pages right on myidentifiers, and copy and paste them everywhere else. I can't stress this enough. Consistency is key!** Especially when it comes to library suppliers ordering your book, and when you come to registering with Lending Rights. If there's an inconsistency between the product description in MyIdentifiers and your printer, you might be rejected when you come to register for Lending Rights!

Thorpe Bowker / myidentifiers is a handy resource for libraries and library suppliers. It's often their 'go to' resource for looking up authors and their books. You'll see where there is space to fill in the year of the author's birth - and death in the case of some authors (whose publishers fill out the forms for them, obviously.)

Side note: Often your book details will appear before the book cover does. I'm not sure why this happens. Book covers are the lost luggage of the literary world.

Nielsen Book Scan is a place librarians and library suppliers often visit as well. It's an excellent idea to get your book titles listed in here:

http://www.nielsenbookscan.com.au

Guess who's got two thumbs and hasn't registered her books with Nielsen Book Sscan yet? This gal!

Yeah, I really need to get on to that as well.

Chapter Five
THE COST OF PRINT RUNS
and postage costs

This is where your brain really gets a work-out. Up until now, it's been 'fill out this form, fill out that form.'

Now you need to do some maths and work out your print book pricing, because this is a business and you want to make a profit out of this exercise.

Whichever printing company you're using, play around with their printing price calculators. Grab a notebook and travel back to high school business maths and all that time you spent looking out the window instead of – Oops, talking about myself again.

When you're looking at printing options, often the printers will have a help page or calculator on their website, so you can work out how much things will cost ahead of time.

Here are some of the helpful pricing calculators from Ingram Spark. (You'll find these by clicking the HELP button on their website.)

As an exercise, I put a 200-page 6x9 paperback into their calculator.

The the total cost of this type of print run would be around $180 - $200, depending on delivery.

Divide this by 30 books = about $6.50 per book.

Not bad!

Playing around with this calculator will give more options. Order more books, the price per book could come down by a few cents each, which all helps. More pages in the book, the cost rises.

POSTAGE

It's very important to think about how much your book will weigh. The more pages, the more it weighs. (Ingram Spark have weight calculators as well.)

A 5x8inch book (which is a regular-sized paperback) will fit in a pre-paid 'Medium C5' envelope from the post office. You can buy these in 10 packs for about $25. That makes them $2.50 each. The maximum weight for these envelopes is 500g.

Which means, if you're posting books individually across Australia, you need to factor in an extra $2.50 per book into your cost price.

However, if the book is more than 250 pages, it won't fit in that envelope. It will be too fat. At this point you either think about reducing the font size of your book, or you go back and edit it one more time to reduce page count.

If you're making a 6x9inch book, which is the size of a *trade paperback*, then you'll need to step up to the 'Large C4 envelope', which is $4.45 each or $42.30 for a pack of 10. I have made this book in this larger format, so I'll be up for higher postage costs. I'll be factoring this into the retail price.

Go to this webpage and work out some calculations. Here is a very long link that was valid at the end of July 2018 https://auspost.com.au/sending/send-within-australia/compare-letter-services/regular-letters-cards

Have a look at parcel bags while you're at it. Parcel bags are pre-paid and good for posting items up to 500g, 3kg and 5kg. There is talk of Australia Post introducing a 1kg bag, but so far no luck.

Play around with the printing price calculators and also play around with formatting your book – you may find a 5x8 paperback is 300 pages, but if you change this format to 6x9, it comes in at 250 pages. That could make a difference to your profit margins.

PRICE HACK:

If you price your books higher, you'll be able to offer a deeper discount, such as 55% (trades love this). Then when you approach the official library suppliers, you can offer them a choice - 55% discount if they order directly from the printer (ie, Ingram etc) or 40% discount if they order from you (to cover postage.)

THOSE OF US WITH TRADITIONAL AND SMALL PRINT PUBLISHERS:

Authors are usually able to buy their titles directly from their publisher for an 'author price'. These purchases won't be counted as a sale, but at least authors can buy them for only a little more than cost price.

If your publisher is in Australia, you'll be up for local postage (which could be considerable.)

Overseas publishers might not charge as much for postage as they may have a special deal with their country's postal service.

In any case, contact your publisher and let them know you're keen to get your books into Australian libraries, and discuss with them the best way forward. (Please keep reading the rest of the book so you will know what else is involved.)

If the publisher is overseas, they'll be happy for you to do this, as it will help create interest in you as an author and they'll see you doing promotions.

If the publisher is Australian, they will be delighted as – get this – Australian publishers also get Lending Rights! It's free money for them, and it can only happen after the author registers for Lending Rights anyway. You'll be doing them a favour and yourself a favour. (This is also why it's super important self-published authors are listed as the publisher because they'll get extra Lending Rights.)

BUT your Australian small publisher may already have a deal in place with a library supplier. What you need to do is contact your publisher and ask them as nicely as possible about how much you'd love to help get get your books into libraries. You want to appear helpful and positive, and show them that you're keen to get your name out there.

If your publisher makes their titles available to library suppliers at trade discount rates, you won't need to worry about pricing or postage as your publisher has this in hand. (Even if they're not very good at it, which is always a possibility.) The key here is not to blunder in and embarrass your publisher or attempt to reinvent the wheel. Because we're all being incredibly professional about this.

No resting on your laurels, published authors. You still need to contact library suppliers to let them know where they can get your book, and you still need to contact libraries and let them know about your book. It's lots of self-promotion, in a good way. So stay tuned, I'll have lots of work for you to do next chapter.

So much work!

Chapter Six

PRICING YOUR BOOKS

How much to charge for paperbacks and ebooks?

Now we get down to the pointy end – What price do you put on your book to make it attractive to library suppliers and libraries, while also delivering you a little profit?

Let's say I set the retail price of my paperback novel at $15.95. (This is the novel I made up in the previous chapter.)

The RRP needs to include GST at some point. Personally, I'm not registered to collect GST, so I can't charge it (oh gawd, I'm talking taxes, somebody shoot me.) But I do have an ABN because I'm a professional. If a library supplier sells my book for $15.95 (unless it's educational non-fiction perhaps?) it will include $1.45 GST, which must go to the government. (ie, $14.50 + 10% GST of $1.45 = $15.95)

(To find the GST portion of your end price, take the total price and divide by 11. That gives you 10% GST. It's like sorcery or something. Or, if you do it the other way round, take your base price and add 10%.)

Maths time!

A $15.95 RRP book might cost $5.96 each to print (based

on our calculations in the last chapter) so we're down to $9.99. (Hardbacks do cost more to print, but they are also much more durable and will cope with being borrowed more times, so you can set the price higher to reflect this.)

If we were hand-selling directly to readers, which I sometimes do, I get a tidy profit. Well done me!

But we're not always hand selling. We're selling to library suppliers, and they'd like to make a little money for their troubles too. No, you can't sell directly to public libraries. Public libraries are local government entities who spend public money, so most only purchase from authorised suppliers. School libraries might make an exception but they too have to answer to their school councils and keep to their budgets, so they would most likely not be able to buy directly from the author.

I put this in to remind authors to please not turn up and sell or donate their books to their local library.

Let's look at this again, offering the library supplier a reasonable discount.

A common discount they'd be interested in would be 40% off the RRP.

40% of $15.95 = $6.38

So, the $15.95 RRP minus the $6.38 discount = $9.57

$9.57 - $5.96 (the cost of the book) = $3.61

$3.61 is still OK as 'profit', but then you have to factor in postage, and postage eats into your profits.

Postage: $2.60

Hooray, you get $1 profit!

This is why it's important to play with your retail price and see if you can offer the 55% discount and still make a small profit. I offer 55% trade discount when library suppliers order directly with Ingram Spark, and 40% when placed with me. I've already had a reply from one supplier to say, 'thanks for that, we'll order from IS.' Another is still happy to order from me. I'm OK with that.

WHERE'S THE PROFIT?

In the Lending Rights!

In years to come, each printed book you have on a public library shelf will earn you about $2 royalty per copy with Public Lending Right (PLR), and you keep getting that PLR for **each year** those books remain on the shelves. Plus, you'll get 30-50c per book as the listed publisher as well. BUT there is a minimum requirement. As of July 2018, it was a minimum of $100 per title. Which is 50 books.

WHAT ABOUT IMMEDIATE PROFIT? I'D LIKE SOME OF THAT PLEASE.

The other option is to increase the RRP of your book so that you can offer deeper trade discounts to library suppliers.

If you think the market will cope, and you've got a cracking story and the covers are magnificently beautiful, then go for it and charge a higher RRP, so you can offer a deeper discount without crippling your bottom line.

Visit a general bookstore and see what their prices are for books that are like yours. Don't compare prices at Big W/Target/K-mart though, their books are heavily, *heavily* discounted and are often 'loss leaders'. You will not be able to compete with them so don't bother.

EBOOK PRICING

Libraries have limited budgets and they need books that will stand the rigours of multiple lendings. Which is why you need to use a good printer with a great reputation.

Ebooks don't have this issue and **just about every library across the country offers ebook lending**. Which is excellent for discoverability.

But library budgets are still limited. If they see your ebook is available to libraries for $9.95, but the general public can get it for $2.99, they might not want your book at all. Yes, the higher library price will make up for the loss of some sales, but your aim is to get your books out there and get them read. Higher prices for libraries could hamper that ambition.

Back Matter

As I said, there's no Lending Right at the moment for ebooks, so if you're getting these into libraries, you'll only be paid for one purchase, even if your books are borrowed heavily.

Think of it as giving your books away to discerning / avid readers who could become superfans down the track. It's vitally important to have back matter that shows the reader who you are, what other books you have, what awards you've won etc. Put in your email address and website and invite them to contact you. Absolutely put in a link to your newsletter list. Not every reader will care, but every now and then one of them will and they will become fans.

Do not put in direct buy links to specific retailers in your back matter, because that can trigger automatic file rejection from retailers.

Ask readers to leave reviews, but don't mention specific places. Phrases like 'please leave a review on Amazon' in your back matter (even when it's not a link) will see the file rejected. The reason it gets rejected is that it upsets all the other retailers who hate seeing the word Amazon in your book (unless you're referring to the geographic region in Brazil).

The best way to get your ebooks into libraries is by making them available to Overdrive.

Overdrive operate in libraries across Australia (and the world) and I'm pretty much in awe of them.

https://www.overdrive.com/libraries

If you're using Draft2Digital to make your ebooks available all over the world, simply select Overdrive on the distribution page and your book will be available for purchase by libraries. Your work, however, is not done, as you still need to do all the promotion (which I will outline in the chapters to come) to let libraries know about your book.

Small Press authors

If you're published with a small press, and your book is available only as an ebook, ask your publisher if your titles are being distributed through Overdrive. That might be all you need to do for ebooks at this stage. However, if you're interested in print runs, ask if your publisher will bring your books out in print – or ask if they'll give you permission to do it yourself. (Check your contract, you may already have the print rights.)

If you're printed with a small press publisher, ask your publisher where library suppliers can order your books from, and what the trade discount is. As I've already mentioned, there are no Lending Right for ebooks (at this stage), which means your ebook-only publisher might not be interested in helping you get your books into libraries. They might even see their ebooks in libraries as a negative, as selling one ebook to a library could be regarded as lost sales to all the people who borrow it instead of buy it.

This is something you'll need to negotiate with your publisher. Good luck!

Publishers love Lending Rights

It has to be the author who registers the books. (I don't make the rules). In other words, the Australian publisher gets free money from all the work you're doing. Harrah! Then again, they took a punt on you and have worn all the costs so far, so it's only right they should get a little extra, down the track.

IF YOUR PUBLISHER IS OVERSEAS:

They may have a similar PLR situation in their country, but as you're not a resident of that country, you can't claim it. I had stacks of books in British Libraries but I couldn't get anything for them as I'm not a resident. Boo Hoo, sucks to be me. But also, the publisher here in Australia, who picked up my book, managed to get my books into plenty of libraries, so, swings and roundabouts.

If your publisher is overseas, contact them about your plans to get the books into libraries here in Australia. Be open and encouraging. Negotiate with them to get a good supply of books - or where the library suppliers can buy them.

YOUR CHECKLIST FOR PART ONE

Have I given you enough work to do?

- Buy ISBNs
- Create a publisher name or use your author name
- Assign one ISBN to each format of your book
- Publish your books (or get ready to publish them)
- Select Overdrive as a distribution option with your ebook distributor
- Work out book prices for your print runs, whether self-published or if you're with a small press
- If you're traditionally published, contact your publisher to discuss your plans to get your titles into Australian libraries
- Work out your postage costs and try not to cry

- Cry anyway

Next, we'll look at all the library suppliers across Australia, how to contact them in a completely professional manner and how to fill in even more online forms!

Plus, it will soon be time to register for those Lending Rights I keep talking about.

PART TWO

Learning all about Lending Rights

Chapter Seven

GETTING READY TO EARN ROYALTIES

A re you ready for another stack of work? Off we go. In part two we'll be:

- Judging books by their covers
- Learning about Lending Rights
- Registering for Lending Rights and filling out online forms
- Putting together a list of Australian library suppliers (for print books)
- Investigating options for ebooks
- Contacting library suppliers - via email and/or by filling in their online forms (yay, more online forms!)
- Creating your own tax invoices (excel spreadsheets galore!)

The online forms will absolutely do your head in after a while, (ooops, talking about myself again) but as you fill them in, you'll make brilliant progress in making your books available to libraries, and that's what this is all about.

Once again I'll be here in the trenches with you.

Sure, Lending Rights don't apply to ebooks - YET - but it's still important to know all of this stuff and be ready to apply for Lending Rights the moment ebooks get the green light. (Please join the ASA and help with the campaign. It's in your own best interests.)

If you're not in print at all, then you won't be contacting Australian library suppliers at this moment - but you need to make sure you're with Overdrive, so your ebooks are getting into libraries that way.

Let's get to work.

Chapter Eight

JUDGING A BOOK BY ITS COVER

We all do it

Whether you can admit it or not, we do judge books by their covers. Personally, you may bristle at this suggestion, determined that you don't; that you always judge a book on its merits. And to that I say, 'Good for you.'

The reason you perhaps take the time to pick up a book – regardless of the cover – and flip it over to read the blurb, even if it's written poorly – and then perhaps open the first page to have a look at the opening few paragraphs that may or may not be very well written . . . is that word starting with T:

Time.

Librarians and library suppliers are busy people who don't have time to mess around. Readers are crunched for time. That means authors can't waste their precious time.

Leave your creative writer brain behind and become a complete professional (remember, they can't see the curry stains on your pyjamas). Being professional starts with an awesome cover. A cover that says, 'This book will be an excellent use of your time.'

Spend some of your time in a book store or library, looking at covers. Go to Amazon and scroll through the top 100 in your favourite category. Be as brutally judgemental as possible. (Privately.) Look at the covers with a critical eye, but also listen to your heart. Does the cover make you sigh? Does it elicit a mood?

Have a look inside the book, at the copyright page and see if the author has acknowledged who created the cover for them. Then look up that cover designer and introduce yourself.

If it's an indie author, they will often acknowledge the cover creator. If it's a big publisher, they might not specifically name the designer, which is annoying.

Check out TheBookDesigner.com and have a scroll through the monthly book cover awards. Some of them are extraordinary and some are just . . . oh dear. If you see a cover you love, think about the feeling it evokes. Magic, emotions, love, passion, fear, intrigue, horror etc. Get a few covers you love and see if your designer can make you a cover that will evokes those.

WARNING: Don't rip-off the artwork. If the cover you love is already pretty famous (or even if it's not) don't make your cover too similar. Not only is it bad form, you could find yourself in legal trouble with copyright claims etc.

Allow me to present the craziest story from YA Twitter in the last year:

The cover artwork *Handbook for Mortals* bore a striking resemblance to, *The Knife Thrower* by artist Gill Del-Mace.

Trust me, you don't want to end up becoming a punchline for shady behaviour.

If you see something you love and want a cover 'like that', just go with the general vibe, OK?

Don't do it yourself. Trust me, unless you're a graphic designer and you really, *REALLY* know what you're doing, do not design your cover yourself.

OK, yes, some people can design a book cover themselves, but it's rare. And you don't want to end up featured in LousyBookCovers.com. Go ahead and waste some time over there. I'm sorry for the metaphorical punch in the face.

HOW TO FIND A COVER DESIGNER?

Ask around. If you see a stunning cover on facebook or twitter, ask the author who the cover artist is. Post questions on social media ask the 'hive mind' for recommendations.

If you're after something super affordable, try checking out websites with ready made ebook covers for about $100 US each. It will give you an idea of what's out there. Again, be brutally judgemental - this is your book baby we're talking about - and see what appeals and appalls.

YOUR COVER NEEDS TO WORK FOR YOU (NOT AGAINST YOU).

The cover will be the first thing librarians see, when you send them a completely professional email (with the sell sheet) about your book. It will also be one of the first things library suppliers see as well. Library suppliers also make their own promotional material to send out to libraries, so the more gorgeous and genre-appropriate your cover, the better your sales are likely to be.

SPINE SPACE

I nearly forgot. Now that your print books are heading towards library shelves, spare a thought for the librarian who needs to catalogue your book. Make space near the base of the spine for a sticker or two. You want readers to find your name quickly, and if your author name is printed all the way down the spine, there will be a sticker over the last few letters, which makes reading your name more difficult.

Spend a little time looking along a library shelf to see what I mean. You might never have noticed this before, but you will now.

Chapter Nine

REGISTERING FOR LENDING RIGHTS

This is the good stuff

Lending Rights came about because of a concerted effort from the Australian Society of Authors (the ASA). Public Lending Rights came into effect in 1975, and Educational Lending Rights in 2000.

The ASA is actively campaigning to have Digital Lending Rights (ebooks and audio books) included.

I'm so grateful to the ASA for their earlier and current campaigns, and I am proud to be a member. You should totally join up, if you're not already.

Lending Rights are managed by the Australian Government Department of Communications and Arts. Here's a really groovy bit from the Public Lending Right Act, 1985.

> **2A Objects of Act**
>
> (a) to make payments to Australian creators of books, and to publishers of books in Australia, in recognition of their loss of income from their books being available for loan from, or for use in, public lending libraries in Australia; and

(b) to support the enrichment of Australian culture by encouraging Australian persons to create books and by encouraging publishers to publish books in Australia.

How about that? It's there to compensate us, and it's there to encourage us to make awesome books and get them into libraries! So really, we should all be doing our patriotic duty as much as possible!

To familiarise yourself, go to this page

https://www.arts.gov.au/funding-and-support/lending-rights

and spend time reading about how Lending Rights work. Most importantly, check whether you're eligible. If you're the co-author, you'll split the Lending Rights with your fellow authors depending on your level of contribution.

IMPORTANT - If you're the sole author, you are eligible for 100% of Lending Right royalties. This often confuses people who are published with small presses who may be on a 10% or 40% royalty deal with that publisher.

Australian citizens and residents are eligible. But guess what? You MUST have an ISBN and it must be officially recorded in an official database - which is why we spent all that time making sure we bought proper ISBNs and they are registered to us as the publisher (where applicable) in an official place of record (ie, Thorpe Bowker or Neilsen Bookscan.)

Now we are going to fill in some online forms.

I first registered for Lending Rights in either 2010 or 2011. So I've previously filled in the details of who I am, and filled in my bank account details.

BUT I also need to register now as a publisher, so claims for the new editions of the Ondine novels (and my future books) come to me as author and as the publisher, while the older editions from Hardie Grant Egmont still come to me as the

GET YOUR BOOK INTO AUSTRALIAN LIBRARIES

author, but to HGE as the publisher. (They have different ISBNs, so that solves any issues there.)

First timers to Lending Rights, start with this online form here:

https://lendingrights.arts.gov.au

The front page will have these two boxes in the top right corner.

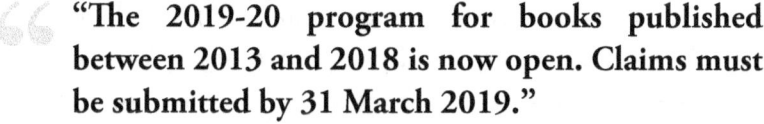

If you're a brand new claimant, click the Register box for new claimants.

If you're a returning claimant, click the 'Sign In' box.

Now, we have some deadlines that must be met.

> **"The 2019-20 program for books published between 2013 and 2018 is now open. Claims must be submitted by 31 March 2019."**

The deadline is always March 31 for the books published the year before. If you miss the deadline, that's OK, you have five years to register your book and you'll still be eligible.

Remember: It's not retrospective. If your book was published in 2015 but you didn't register until 2019, then you've missed those years of royalties. However, you will continue to collect royalties for as many years as your books are on shelves (in sufficient numbers, which at the moment is 50) in libraries.

If this is all too tricky (and it can be confusing) There are helplines you can call, so someone can hold your hand and walk you through it.

UPDATE! (June 8, 2018) They are so helpful! I had a call a couple of weeks ago from a lovely chap at the Lending Rights office. Yes, he called me! Guess what dopey thing I'd done? I'd registered as a publisher (for all my self-published books) and then hadn't filled in my titles! There was an issue with the connection between my registration as an author and publisher, which he fixed so quickly so they were linked, and off I went. Thank you!

MATCH YOUR CATEGORIES

Not only will you need to make sure the ISBN is spot on, and your titles are correctly matched; you'll need to make sure your book description is the same. Otherwise you'll get 'computer says no' treatment. Maintain consistency with correct titles, description, ISBN, publisher, keywords/categories. If there's a mismatch, Lending Rights will query your 'MARC'. MARC stands for **Ma**chine **R**eadable **C**ataloguing record, and it will burn your noggin.

You will need to give Lending Rights your bank account details. The money is electronically deposited once a year, in early to mid-June. The money is considered taxable income, PS, so make sure you keep good records (for those of us earning enough to pay tax.)

The website can be slow to load, especially when it's close to the deadline for registering books. If the slow speed drives you mad, log off and have a cup of tea (or something stronger) and come back later and try again.

> *Reminder: you have several years to register each title and its corresponding ISBN, but you only get paid for the years* after *you register (it doesn't work retrospectively). If your book came out in 2014 but you only registered for it in 2016, you won't see money for those two years between 2014 and 2016, only the years that follow. The earlier you register, the more you'll get.*

GET YOUR BOOK INTO AUSTRALIAN LIBRARIES

Australian Government
Department of Communications and the Arts

Contact Us

Sign In   Redeem Invitation

Existing Claimant sign in

| Claimant Number | 309291 |
| Password | •••••••••••••••• |

☐ Remember me?

[Sign in]   Forgot Your Password?

When you're the author AND the publisher, you are eligible for *publisher payments* as well. It's not as much as the author gets - I think it averages out to 30 or 50c or something - but it's a lovely little top-up and you deserve it.

That's is why you need to get a proper ISBN where you can be listed as the publisher. Noooooow it's all making sense, right?

Another thing about Lending Rights. They are broken up into separate Public Lending Rights (for public libraries) and Educational Lending Rights (for school libraries). You need to 'earn' a minimum $100 in royalties for each title, about 50 copies, otherwise you get nothing. (Here, have a tissue.) My most recent statement showed only 10 copies of one of my recent titles, so I earned nothing for that one. (But I had nearly 300 of another title, so that made up for it!)

What's worse, Lending Rights for that low-number don't 'roll over' to the following year either.

I also wouldn't be surprised if they raise this minimum to $150 soon. Grumble, mumble.

The next image is really important. It's your Title Claim. Don't stress that you can't read the tiny print. I'm merely showing these images as an illustration of what you'll be looking for when you register your titles.

Title Claim

Creator title claim for : 309291

Please note:
- to be eligible to receive a payment, you must be entitled to receive a royalty payment for the sale of this book.
- No MARC record books, books older than five years, EBooks, online resources, magazines, serials, CDs, audio books, activity books, single use books (e.g. workbooks, colouring-in books) are ineligible to claim.

Are you self publishing this title claim? Yes

If you are an eligible creator and publishing your own book, then you will need to register as a self publisher. You will also need to submit a Title Claim for both your Creator and Publisher IDs.

Details of ISBNs for this edition of the title	ISBN	Book Form	Year of Publication (yyyy)
	9780995383951	Printed	2016
		Printed	
		Printed	
		Printed	
		Printed	

Click here to validate book details

ISBN validation is complete.

Book Title	Robyn and the Hoodettes
Publisher's Name	Ebony McKenna
Place of Publication	[Australia]
Your name or a pseudonym as shown on the title page	Ebony McKenna
What was your contribution to this title?	Author
Do you receive royalties from the sale of this title?	Yes
What is your percentage entitlement to the royalties?	100 (%)

Payments are calculated based on the royalty split of each eligible creator. If you are the sole creator, enter your royalty split as 100%. If there is more than one eligible creator, list your royalty split out of 100%. For example, if there are two creators, and you receive 7.5% and the other receives 2.5%, you enter 75%. If there are three creators who receive an equal royalty split, then you enter 33.33%. For Self...

Don't stress if you make a mistake. You can call the lovely people at Lending Rights - using the contact details on the website - and they will help out. Just stay calm, lovely and polite and it will all work out.

IMPORTANT INFORMATION

Many authors get confused when it comes to claiming the percentage of royalties for lending rights.

It has nothing to do with the royalty rate you might have with your publisher.

If you're the only author - you're entitled to 100% of the Lending Rights Royalties.

This often confuses some authors who mix this section up with the royalty rate they're getting from their *publisher* for book sales, which can be as miserable as 4% but is usually somewhere around 10%. Yes, I'm repeating myself because this is important.

For a Lending Right claim, you're getting 100%. Unless you've co-authored. If there are two of you, you're claiming 50% each and if there are 3 of you 33% and so on. However, if one of you has done the bulk of the work, then you may need to claim a 60-40 or 70-30 split instead.

The smallest amount you can claim is 20%. **This means there can be no more than five overall contributors**. This could be five authors, or four authors and an illustrator etc. I'm pretty sure it does not include the editor, unless the editor is also a direct contributor. (For example, an editor who also contributes a story in an anthology.) If you're not sure, then please contact Lending Rights to get confirmation.

Once you're done, click the teeensy little 'I agree' box and submit your claim!

The sooner you get on to it, the better. My first book, *Ondine*, hit shelves in 2010. I registered straight away and started getting ELR (Education Lending Right) and PLR (Public Lending Right) in 2012 and it was marvellous. Close to $500 for just one book across both lending rights. I was rapt. In 2011 I added *The Autumn Palace* into Lending Rights and from 2013 my royalties grew. The royalties stayed high for several years, which showed me just how valuable Lending Rights were. (It also proved my books were on library shelves for years. Books don't stay on the shelves if they're not getting borrowed.)

UPDATE: May 31, 2018, I've just received the paperwork from the Lending Rights department. This is for books that were in libraries in 2016 - which is quite the lag time! Happily for me, the number of my 'old' titles on shelves has grown. This doesn't include all the hard work I have been doing during 2017 and 2018 to get more of my books out there into libraries. I can't wait to see what next year's report shows.

My point being, yes, this is a lot of work. Loads of forms to fill in and you might not end up getting all that much for a few years. BUT it's there, it builds every year, so you may as well take your slice of the pie.

Chapter Ten

DEADLINES FOR LENDING RIGHTS

You have five years in which to register your book, from the time it was first published. If it was published more than five years ago, you can't register for Lending Rights for that particular title with its that ISBN. (Even if that particular book is still on library shelves.)

The answer to this situation is to publish a new edition, with a new ISBN. Then you'll need to start the process of marketing that new edition to library suppliers and libraries again.

Once your new book is registered for Lending Rights, it doesn't 'expire', as long as it's still on library shelves in enough numbers.

As an example, my books that were published in 2010 were still earning Lending Rights in 2018.

You have until March 31 2019 to register books published in 2018, which will be paid the following year, so June 2020. It's basically a two-year turnaround.

There is no penalty for registering 'early', so you may as well register your book as soon as it's published, then you don't have to worry about it again.

Remember, you can only register book titles for Lending Rights once you've registered the ISBN in a recognised database, like Thorpe Bowker's myidentifiers.

I'm repeating myself, because this needs repeating. Make sure all your data for each title is the same - on myidentifiers, with your printer and elsewhere. If for some reason the Lending Rights Claim won't register, and that word 'MARC' comes up, double check your ISBN details with the printer - make sure all the categories and descriptions are identical. Make sure the title is consistent. Go through line by line if you need to.

Chapter Eleven

AUSTRALIAS BIG LIBRARY SUPPLIERS

The main players in public and school library suppliers in Australia are:

James Bennett - NSW based

http://www.bennett.com.au/contact

Noodle around on their website, they have information for small-presses and self-published authors.

Peter Pal - Qld based

http://www.peterpal.com.au

WestBooks - WA based

http://www.westbooks.com.au

ALS Library Services - SA based

https://www.alslib.com.au

DLS - Vic based

http://www.dlsbooks.com

These are the big five I've been dealing with. (Along with some smaller suppliers and independent bookstores who sell directly into schools.)

In many cases, you'll need to send an email introducing yourself and your book titles. Then they'll get back to you, usually in a few days.

Once you've done that, you'll most likely need to fill out the supplier's own online information forms about each title. Huzzah, more online forms!

Although there's basically one big supplier in each state, they don't have a monopoly in those states. That means even if you've only made contact with James Bennett, they still supply books to libraries across Australia (and New Zealand). But not every library. For what it's worth, your titles may as well be listed with all the suppliers.

My best relationship has been with ALS in South Australia. They are so completely lovely, and they're keen to hear from self-published authors.

Here's how it works:

- I visit a supplier's website
- Email them or fill in the forms to register my books with them, along with ISBNs, covers, blurbs, dimensions, weight etc.
- Register the retail prices including GST, and the trade discounts they would receive - the pricing we worked out earlier comes into effect here.
- Once the titles are in the supplier's system, I then contact libraries directly and let them know my book is available from the official suppliers.
- A few weeks to a few months later, the suppliers get orders from libaries. They either order directly from the printer (Ingram Spark) or contact me via email with an order for books.

Here's where you need to get really organised (big shout out to everyone with ADHD. #TheStruggleIsReal)

You'll need to keep records of which companies you've contacted - and any website logins and passwords to re-access when your next book comes out. The more work you do, and the less work they have to do, the more professional you will appear.

Take your time to look over these main five suppliers' websites. Click on their pages to see what they do (they do a lot!). Once your books are in with these library suppliers, you're really on your way.

You're in the big time now!

EBOOKS

The big one for library distrubution of ebooks is Overdrive. Many libraries are using this ebook retailer to stock their virtual shelves. There are others, so look them up. Google is your friend.

The easiest way I've found to get 'in' with Overdrive is to use Draft2Digital (D2D) to load my books onto retailer websites including Overdrive as a retailer.

Smashwords too will publish your ebook to Overdrive, and many others, provided it meets the 'Premium catalogue' requirements. (Basically no glitches or issues which annoy all the other retailers). Please read the relevant section on this page for more up-to-date information:

https://www.smashwords.com/dashboard/channelManager/

If you're using Smashwords to upload your titles to the world, you're all set to see your books for sale to libraries through **Library Direct, Baker & Taylor's Axis360, Gardners, OverDrive, Bibliotheca and Odilo.**

Ebook formatters and aggregators like Smashwords and Draft2Digital have made it easier than ever for indie and small press authors to sell their ebooks all over the world, and sell them to libraries.

BUT

You as the author still need to let the libraries know your books are available, so get ready to make sell sheets and be totes profesh about it.

Again, if you are with a small press and you want to make sure your books are available to libraries, check with your publisher to see what sales channels they are going to sell through (if it's in your contract) or ask your editor on which sales platforms your books are sold. Sorry if I'm repeating myself, but if you're with a small press you need to be businesslike and keep in contact - don't assume they'll do the work for you. (Note the problem - 'I'd like to be in libraries' - then give them the solution - 'I know how to do this, make it available in Overdrive' etc.)

Chapter Twelve

CONTACTING LIBRARY SUPPLIERS

The first contact you'll have with a library supplier is online. As a new supplier, you'll need to have all your information at hand - your ABN, book details, banking details etc. You need an ABN so they can put you into their system as a supplier. Without an ABN, you're going to give them tax withholding headaches and you won't appear professional.

Side note:
If you don't have an ABN, it's easy to get one - plus, they're free. Have your Tax File number handy and log on to the ATO website at www.ato.gov.au. Then follow the links to getting your Australian Business Number. I'm fairly sure you'll need to quote your ABN when you register with printers and ebook retailers anyway.

When you contact the library supplier, it will probably be via their 'contact us' email. So send them an email introducing yourself.

SAMPLE INTRO EMAIL

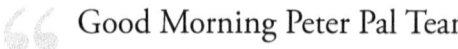
Good Morning Peter Pal Team,

I'm [state your real name] an Australian author with [number of] books in print under the writing name of [my writing name].

[A paragraph here about your titles.] (Or something like this which shows you're a professional. Being kind and nice is always a good way to start, but let's not get too buttery.)

As a self-published author/author with a small press, I have a good supply of titles available - list where they can purchase your titles and what the discount is.

Please let me know the most convenient way I can list my titles with you.

Yours faithfully,

my name here.

Obviously you will do a much better job when you come to do this for real. Each library supplier has a different way to list new titles. Do it their way each time. Make their lives as easy as possible.

BIC CATEGORIES

Some library suppliers' forms will ask for "BIC Categories." to classify your book. BIC means Book Industry Communication. Go here https://ns.editeur.org/bic_categories and find the categories that match your book.

Chapter Thirteen

INVOICES

For the times you'll be handling sales yourself

It's brilliant if library suppliers go straight to your printer to get stock, that way you don't have to handle the sales and invoices. But if they do want to deal directly with you, get ready.

They will most likely email an order of books to you, but sometimes you'll get snail mail.

Get the order together and send it off promptly with your invoice.

Your invoice needs to include:

- ABN
- Date
- Library Supplier's Order Number (so they can match it to their ordering records.)
- Number of titles ordered and the ISBNs of those titles
- Full RRP cost of the books
- Cost of titles to the library supplier - which shows the discount
- Total cost the supplier needs to pay

- If you're registered for GST, put GST on it.
- If not, don't put GST.
- Provide your bank account details because you want to get paid, right?

When sending books, you want them to arrive in perfect condition.

I wrap them in something light but firm, so it doesn't add to the weight! A manilla folder keeps the books steady and protects them from bashing around into each other in transit.

If it's an order for one book (this happens sometimes) I grin and bear it and send it off. If it's a few books, I wrap them carefully with a smile.

If it's an order for ten or more books (and I extra LOVE when that happens), then sometimes it's easier to order the books from the printer - and get them delivered straight to the library supplier.

(There are places where you can change delivery addresses within the printers' websites.)

If you do this, send the supplier an email explaining that the books will be coming directly from the printer. You won't be able to put your invoice in with those books, so email them your invoice and make sure all the details are there so they can match the invoice with the books, when the books arrive.

Side Note: If you don't already have a template for a tax invoice - either conduct a quick Google search for free invoice templates, or play around with excel and make one. It doesn't need stunning graphics, it just needs to be clear.

It bears repeating, don't charge extra GST unless you're registered to collect it. Once you are registered to collect GST, you have to charge GST for everything unless it's 'educational' which

I assume is non-fiction maybe? I really am not sure. I can't imagine my non-fiction would be seen as 'educational' in the strict sense, unless a secondary or tertiary institution put it on their syllabus.

Don't charge extra postage unless you've previously stated you'll be doing that. It's just a personal thing, but I like to know how much I'm up for when I buy things online, and I don't like surprises. That's why we did all the calculations earlier, so that you could include postage in the price of your books - or at least indicate what the postage would be.

YOUR NEW CHECKLIST

You have a fair bit to go on with now.

- Make sure your covers are brilliant - chase down your favourite designers and get the best cover for your book.
- Register for Lending Rights.
- Draft a professional introduction for contacting library suppliers.
- Get an ABN (if you don't already have one).
- Create your own tax invoices and templates for when the orders come in.

Next part we'll be creating Sell Sheets and contacting libraries to let them know where they can order your books!

PART THREE

Promoting your books to libraries

Chapter Fourteen
SELL SHEETS

This part will focus on the vital tasks of making sell sheets to promote your books and making contact with public and school libraries (If your books are sutable for schools)

Our three important jobs are:

- Creating Sell sheets
- Creating Library lists
- Contacting Libraries

What is a sell sheet anyway?

It's a standard size (usually A4) page containing an image of your book cover, with lovely promotional words around them. Waaaay back when I was published with Egmont in the UK, they would send sell sheets with Advance Reader Copies (ARCs) of the book, out to reviewers. They also would have sent these sell sheets out to library suppliers across the UK, because soon after my book came out, I couldn't help googling and *pure joy* there was my book, ready to borrow all over the British Isles.

You need to make one of these sell sheets, which will give

librarians who open your email an instant idea of your book and more importantly your targeted readership.

A sell sheet will need

- A beautiful, high-resolution image of your book cover.
- An enticing blurb indicating the target readership and what the story is about.
- A short author bio. SHORT!
- Book measurements and ISBN (ie, paperback, size format, number of pages etc).
- Author contact details should the library invite you to give talks or workshops.

Turn the page to see one I've prepared earlier.

GET YOUR BOOK INTO AUSTRALIAN LIBRARIES

You can put in a author photo on your sell sheet if you like. This sell sheet looks amazing in colour - and as you'll be sending these out in emails, the colour really pops. In a paperback with black and white printing? Not so much.

Another handy graphic device to use is to take elements from your cover design and have that repeat in your sell sheet.

For 1916-ish, I used the image layer of the soldiers and the sky background. It's important to be able to separate the layers so you can put all your text on a 'clean' background. Text over text (even if you blur the text) ends up looking messy.

A free tool you can use to both make covers and make sell sheets is Canva (www.canva.com). They have templates and existing designs you can alter, to make something pretty.

But what if you don't have the design chops to do make

something even close to these sell sheets?

You could ask your cover designer to make a 'sell sheet' for your book.

1. The Summer of Shambles   ISBN 978-0-9953839-1-3   207 pages

This first book in the ONDINE quartet is filled with adventure, fairytale romance and magical fun. At Psychic Summercamp, fifteen-year-old Ondine doubts she possesses her family's magical abilities. But when her pet ferret Shambles starts talking - in a cheeky Scottish accent no less - anything seems possible. Is Shambles really a young man trapped in a witch's curse, as he claims? And what terrible crime did he commit to deserve such punishment? While Ondine tries to untangle the truth about Shambles, the pair uncover a plot to assassinate a royal family member and unlock the secret to a long-lost treasure. Amongst all this intrigue and mayhem, can Ondine overcome her self-doubts and save the day?

2. The Autumn Palace   ISBN 978-0-9953839-2-0   253 pages

This second sassy adventure in the ONDINE quadrilogy combines fairytale romance with magical fun. Detective duo Ondine and her handsome new boyfriend Hamish - who has a talent for transforming into a ferret - have landed themselves a dangerous mission from The Duke of Brugel. Upon entering the palace grounds they are confronted by a fierce tornado that awakens something dark and ominous. Unexplained phenomena begin intruding on every day life at an alarming rate. Surrounded by strange magic, Ondine and Hamish must expose a royal conspiracy, champion the palace's downtrodden servants and solve a baffling mystery. With so much at stake, will they ever find time for their burgeoning romance to blossom?

Or, you could do a search for 'sell sheet templates' and put your book elements in the spaces made by the template (which is what I did for 1916-ish)

Or, if you simply want to write a blurb about what's in your book, keep things simple and opt for a plain sheet with clearly set-out information blocks, like the image on the previous page: These were for the four-book Ondine series. The covers are already colourful and packed with detail. Putting them on a colourful background would make everything too busy. Far easier to simply place them on the white page with all the details a collections librarian will need, when considering whether to order them in for readers.

Your sell sheet must at the very least contain your book's ISBN, page count, a cover, target readership and where it can be purchased.

Extra infomation can include book dimensions and more information about the author - although keep this brief.

The cover has to do a LOT of work (as it should) because it has to get approval from a lot of gatekeepers to get through to the library shelves.

It needs to appeal to library suppliers so they will list the books.

It needs to appeal to collection librarians so they will buy your books. (Collection librarians are the ones who are in charge of curating the collections, ps.)

The cover then needs to appeal to readers who are in an actual library, surrounded by everyone else's books and their stunning covers.

Give the reader a reason to choose your book over all the others.

A sell sheet is a lot of work and you need to get it right.

EBOOK AUTHORS

You still need to make sell sheets as well, so that you can show them to librarians across this beautiful country.

Your ebook may already be in Overdrive or Biblio - well done - but the busy collections managers and librarians have so many ebooks to choose from, they might not have seen yours yet.

Make sell sheets and email them out to libraries to let them know about your book/s.

Keep it fresh, simple and easy to read. Make your cover pop! Woot!

Are you thinking your cover might not be 'strong' enough to really pop? That's OK. Go back to chapter 8 and have a read through, making note of all the places where you could get a new cover designer.

Even established authors who are traditionally published get new covers from time to time. It's a way to refresh to books and give them some new attention. Tastes and styles change all the time. Sometimes a new, professional cover, can help your book work that little bit harder and make the difference between libraries ordering your book or not.

Chapter Fifteen
CREATING LIBRARY LISTS

Now we're going to create a huge list of all the libraries to contact. You don't have to contact every single one by any means. But it's a handy list - AND next time you're planning a holiday, maybe visit a couple of libraries in the region you're going to. That's always fun.

The focus here is on contacting public libraries.

SCHOOL LIBRARIES

Young Adult and Middle Grade authors should also make a separate list of all the primary and high schools in your area, so you can contact them and let them know you're a local author, available for school visits etc. (And get a Working With Children Check.)

Honestly time:

I have failed spectacularly at this. Sure, I've emailed many high schools on my side of Melbourne, but not one has contacted me directly. Why? Because their funds are so limited. For a start, many primary schools don't have dedicated librarians. But the biggest problem is the school library needs to stick to its budget. They simply can't buy the all books they want to.

School libraries also have speaker agencies contacting them all the time about people available to give school talks. I've also tried a few times to get listed with speaker agencies. I'll keep trying that one as well.

WORKING WITH CHILDREN CHECK

If you're planning on stepping foot inside a primary or secondary school, get a Working With Children Check. This link www.workingwithchildren.vic.gov.au takes you to the Victorian site (my home state). If you're outside Victoria, go to your favourite search engine and type 'working with children check' and add your home state to the search.

How else to be invited into schools?

Pester power from students. When students start bugging their librarians about an amazing author they love, they're more likely to invite them in. They'll listen to their students more than 'some random author'.

School librarians are, by nature, wonderful people who have a deep and abiding love for books. They visit public libraries all the time.

If your books are in the local public libraries, local students (and school librarians) will see them there and borrow them. Then they'll rave about the books to their friends and hassle their school librarians to get them in. That's the word of mouth magic going on. It can take a very long time for this to happen, by the way.

As a real-life example: Over Christmas 2017, a student (who used to be at primary school with my son) told me she'd requested her high school get my books in. I thanked her profusely (even though I hadn't received any orders lately.) Then I checked my sales on Blurb and lo, an order had gone through for one of each title in early December. Wonderful! (Although I haven't been invited to speak, so I should get in touch.)

CHECKING ON YOUR BOOKS:

If you've previously been published, check where your books might already be by going to https://trove.nla.gov.au and search for your writing name.

(Ego surfing is the best!)

You never know what will show up in a catalogue somewhere, especially if you've been writing for a few decades.

If you see some libraries that have your books, put them at the top of your 'libraries to contact' list when you have a new book out.

Then it's time to travel all over the countryside.

TASMANIA

Starting here first is easy, because all public libraries in Tasmania come under the LINC umbrella, which makes them easy to contact.

Go here and suggest your book title to them and which suppliers they can buy from - and LINC will do the rest.

https://www.linc.tas.gov.au

There is a form to suggest a book, but you need your borrower number - which means unless you're local, you can't do it as you won't have a library card. (Plus, it probably stops authors pretending to be locals and filling it in . . . ooops.)

Try this email address and introduce yourself professionally and courteously. libraries.tas@education.tas.gov.au

Again, check their catalogue to make sure your title isn't already there. Tell them all about your new ones too.

The bonus for contacting LINC is that it's one service to cover the whole state. When they reply to your query, you can email them your book's beautiful sell sheet.

VICTORIA

Type this link in and feast your eyes on this magnificent page:
https://www.localgovernment.vic.gov.au/public-libraries/find-your-local-library

Scroll down, keep scrolling, and you'll see every public library and Mechanics' Institute in the state, complete with phone numbers, addresses and emails.

For these libraries, you will need your sell sheets, and plenty of patience as you contact each library individually, via email. As much as possible, tailor each email specifically to that council or regional library. (You may have been born there, or worked there, or live there now.) Bonus, some shires and local councils have doubled or tripled up, creating a regional library service that covers a dozen libraries across multiple local councils. You only need to contact one librarian in each of those regions, not each individual library. The larger library services usually have someone dedicated to your type of book (ie, a youth librarian for younger readers, and a collections manager for general fiction etc.)

SOUTH AUSTRALIA

OK, this one's a bit more legwork, but a real treasure trove. There's a page here to find every single public library, so what you do is click on each library symbol and the contact details pop up
http://www.libraries.sa.gov.au/page.aspx?u=5

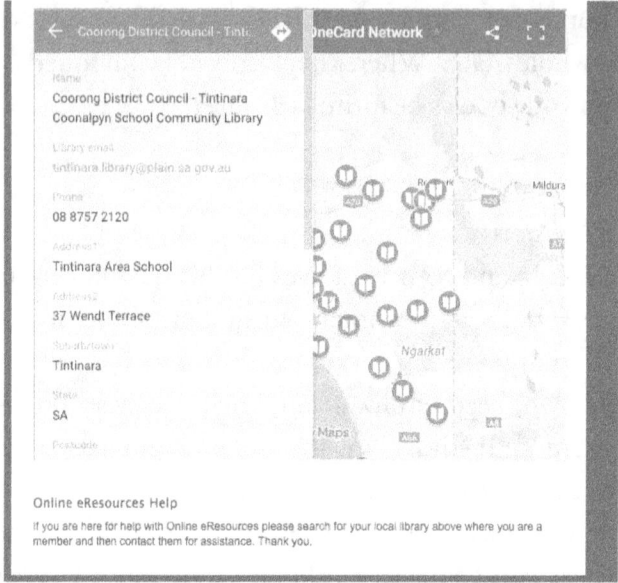

How cute is that?

Again, before making contact, use SA Libraries' catalogue checker here:

https://onecard.network/client/en_AU/sapubliclibraries to see if any of your earlier published books are already on the shelves. This will give you the entire catalogue for the whole state. Hooray!

WESTERN AUSTRALIA

Starting with ebooks, let's look at Overdrive - it's all over WA because of the vast distances between some towns. This is why ebooks have become so important to libraries - especially those with tight budgets and vast areas to cover.

Type your author name in the search engine link below - and see what books come up.

https://wapldmc.overdrive.com

There's scope here to recommend four titles every month. My

four Ondines show up in the search - so I can recommend them (and choose which library they should go to). That's pretty excellent. Then next month I'll recommend my other titles.

For those of us with paperbacks, we're in for the internet version of 'wearing out shoe leather'.

Many of the smaller and remote libraries rely on book supplies from the State Library of Western Australia, so that's an excellent place to start.

State Library of Western Australia
info@slwa.wa.gov.au

I just checked my name and 13 copies of my books are in the State Library's catalogue, which fills me with glee. Even better, all four Ondine's are at a library called Success Public Library. Success? YES!

OK, let's have a look at some of the public libraries across Australia's biggest state.

City Of Melville
library@melville.wa.gov.au

Albany Public Library
library@albany.wa.gov.au

City of Swan (six libraries in all, these are the main ones)
altone.library@swan.wa.gov.au
midland.library@swan.wa.gov.au
ellenbrook.library@swan.wa.gov.au
bullsbrook.library@swan.wa.gov.au

City of Gosnells
Four libraries Amherst Village Library, Kenwick Library, Gosbell's Knowledge Centre and Thornlie Library
Library_queries@gosnells.wa.gov.au

City of Armidale
armadale.library@armadale.wa.gov.au

Shire of Augusta Margaret River
amrlibrary@amrshire.wa.gov.au

Shire of Harvey
Harvey Library
hstaff@harvey.wa.gov.au
Australind library
astaff@harvey.wa.gov.au
Yarloop Library and Binningup Library
ystaff@harvey.wa.gov.au
Shire of Dandaragan (four libraries)
 jblibrary@dandaragan.wa.gov.au
cervanteslibrary@dandaragan.wa.gov.au
dandaraganlibrary@westnet.com.au
badgingarralibrary@westnet.com.au
City of Rockingham
Mary Davies Library and Community Centre
mdlcccontact@rockingham.wa.gov.au
Rockingham Central Library
rclcontact@rockingham.wa.gov.au
The Shire of Donnybrook Balingup
Donnybrook Balingup Library services
Teacher/Community Librarian: Esme Kidd
Shire Library Officer: Margaret Evans
No email but a website form in this page to make contact http://www.donnybrook-balingup.wa.gov.au/contact/
Bassendean Public Library
baslib@bassendean.wa.gov.au
City of Bayswater, 3 Libraries
http://www.bayswater.wa.gov.au/library/contact-your-library
Shire of Mt Marshall
Beacon, WA (Librarian in attendance Tuesdays 9am to 3.30pm, sounds adorable!)
Online contact form
http://www.beaconwa.com.au/contact-page.html
Bencubbin Public Library

admin@mtmarshall.wa.gov.au

City of Belmont

Ruth Faulkner Public Library, Belmont

libinfodesk@belmont.wa.gov.au

City of Canning

4 libraries; Bentley Library Cannington Library, Riverton Library, Willetton Library.

libraryservices@canning.wa.gov.au

Shire of Beverley

Please contact either Sheridan Irvine, Mary Jones or Taleeya Scott at library@beverley.wa.gov.au

Bidyadanga Community Library

The recognised traditional owners of the land are the Karajarri people. Bidyadanga is the largest remote Aboriginal community in Western Australia with a population of approximately 750 residents and is home to the Karajarri, Juwalinny, Mangala, Nyungamarta and Yulpartja language groups.

enquiries@baclg.org.au

Shire of Broome

library@broome.wa.gov.au

Shire of Chittering

Bindoon Library

chatter@chittering.wa.gov.au This is the email to volunteer at the library. Bindoon also has a prominent note about using Overdrive for ebooks, which is an excellent use of their resources.

ONE LIBRARY

Many libraries are also using a service called One Library to help manage resources

"The new Shire of Boddington Library has joined with 11 other local governments in a new, sharing Library Management

System, which will give library members access to a larger supply of resources.

What is One Library?

The One Library network is the first of its kind in Western Australia,

connecting 25 Libraries over the South West; giving greater access to the

community. You will be able to use your new Library card to borrow and return items at any of the participating Libraries.

City of Bunbury, Shire of Capel, Shire of Dardanup, Shire of Harvey, Shire of Waroona, Shire of Boyup Brook, City Of Busselton, Shire of Manjimup, Shire of Bridgetown-Greenbushes, Shire of Donnybrook- Balingup, Shire of Nannup and the Shire of Boddington.

I'd suggest contacting either of these two main libraries within the One Library collective:

Bunbury Library
bunlib@bunbury.wa.gov.au
Shire of Boddington
Boddington Public Library
library@boddington.wa.gov.au

* * *

Shire of Mundaring
Albert Facey Memorial Library
Mundaring - 9290 6780 mills@mundaring.wa.gov.au
Katharine Susannah Prichard Library
Boya - 9290 6755
gills@mundaring.wa.gov.au
Shire of Capel
Couldn't find any direct way to contact the library, so try this
info@capel.wa.gov.au

Shire of Jerramungup
Jerramungup Library
Community Resource Centre, Tobruk Road
Librarian: Sharon Baldwin
Email: jcrc.library@jerramungupcrc.com.au
Bremer Bay Library
Community Resource Centre, Mary Street
Manager: Naomi Hall
Librarian:
Suzanne Hill
Email: library@bremerbaycrc.com
Shire of Brookton
The Brookton Public Library is operated by the Brookton Community Resource Centre.
brookton@crc.net.au
Broomehill Public Library
BHVCounter@shirebt.wa.gov.au
Shire of Bruce Rock
No direct contact for the library so try this:
admin@brucerock.wa.gov.au
City of Bunbury
bunlib@bunbury.wa.gov.au
Busselton Public Library
library@busselton.wa.gov.au
Shire of Victoria Plains
Bolgart Hills
bolgartlibrary@victoriaplains.wa.gov.au
Calingiri
csolibrary@victoriaplains.wa.gov.au
Town of Cambridge
library@cambridge.wa.gov.au
Shire of Carnamah
shire@carnmah.wa.gov.au

eneabba.library@westnet.com.au
Shire of Carnarvon
library.staff@carnarvon.wa.gov.au
Christmas Island Shire
Christmas Island Public Library
OMG Christmas Island! Brilliant
susan@shire.gov.cx
Town of Claremont
library@claremont.wa.gov.au
City of Wanneroo (four libraries)
Clarkson Library
Clarksonl@wanneroo.wa.gov.au
Girrawheen Library
Wanneroo Library
Yanchep/Two Rocks Library
City of Cockburn
Use their Cockburn Libraries contact form here
https://www.cockburnlibraries.com.au/about-us/contact-maps-hours/cockburn-libraries-contact-form/
Cocos Islands
Cocos Islands Community Resource Centre
cocosislands@crc.net.au

Because if your books aren't in the middle of the Indian Ocean, you're not really trying, are you? We should totally have a competition, first person to show me their books in the Cocos Island library wins my entire catalogue of ebooks!

Shire of Collie
library@collie.wa.gov.au
Coolgardie Shire Council
Kambalda Community Recreation Facility
library@coolgardie.wa.gov.au
Shire of Coorow
(3 Libraries, Coorow Public Library, Leeman Public Library

and Green Head Public Library
leeman@coorow.wa.gov.au
Shire of Peppermint Grove
The Grove Public Library
library@thegrovelibrary.com
Cranbrook Public Library
cranbrookpubliclibrary@gillamii.org.au
Cue Public Library
shire@cue.wa.gov.au
City of Karratha
Dampier Public Library
Karratha Public Library
Local History Office
Roebourne Public Library
Wickham Public Library
karratha.library@karratha.wa.gov.au
Shire of Dardanup
(Dardanup and Eaton libraries)
elibrary@dardanup.wa.gov.au
Darkan Public Library (administered by the West Arthur Community Resource Centre)
westarthur@crc.net.au
Denmark Public Library
Voted Australia's Favourite Library 2014
library@denmark.wa.gov.au
Shire of Derby / West Kimberley
No specific email for the library but here is a contact email for the shire.
sdwk@sdwk.wa.gov.au
City of Sterling
Daniella Public Library
Dianella.Library@stirling.wa.gov.au
Inglewood

Inglewood.Library@stirling.wa.gov.au
Karinyup
Karrinyup.Library@stirling.wa.gov.au
Shire of Irwin
Dongara Public Library
library@irwin.wa.gov.au
Dowerin Public Library
(Dowerin community resource centre)
dowerin@crc.net.au
Dumbleyung
library@dumbleyung.wa.gov.au
City of Joondalup
Duncraig Public Library
Joondalup
joondalup.library@joondalup.wa.gov.au
Whitford
Woodvale
Esperance Public Library
library@esperance.wa.gov.au
Exmouth Public Library
records@exmouth.wa.gov.au
City of Mandurah
Mandurah Library
manlib @mandurah.wa.gov.au
Fitzroy Crossing Public Library
fxlibrary@sdwk.wa.gov.au
City of Kalamunda
Kalamunda Library:
Forrestfield Library:
Lesmurdie Library:
High Wycombe Library:
libraries@kalamunda.wa.gov.au
Shire of Cranbrook

Cranbrook Public Library
Frankland Public Library
shire@cranbrook.wa.gov.au
Fremantle City Library
(Lots of changes to council buildings and some demolition going on. But the grand opening should be epic.)
frelib@fremantle.wa.gov.au
Gascoyne Junction Community Resource Centre
crc@uppergascoyne.wa.gov.au
City of Greater Geraldton
Mullewa Public Library
Geraldton Regional Library
library@cgg.wa.gov.au
Shire of Gingin
Gingin Public Library
mail@gingin.wa.gov.au
Shire of Gnowangerup
Gnowangerup Public Library
gnplib@wn.com.au
Officers:Olivia Letter & Jo Davies
Ongerup Library and Post Office
onglib@westnet.com.au
Shire of Goomalling
Goomalling Public Library (part of the Goomalling Community Centre
goomalling@crc.net.au
Shire of Halls Creek
Halls Creek Public Library
hcshire@hcshire.wa.gov.au
Hopetoun Public Library
hopetoun@crc.net.au
Includes local and state library stock amongst their 3,500 books.

Shire of Kondinin
Kondinin Public Library
kndlibrary@kondinin.wa.gov.au
Hyden Public Library
hylib@kondinin.wa.gov.au
Jerramungup Public Library
Librarian: Sharon Baldwin
jcrc.library@jerramungupcrc.com.au
Kalgoorlie-Boulder Public Library
(William Grundt Memorial Library)
mailbag@ckb.wa.gov.au

I don't know about you, but I'm going crosseyed at the list so far. I feel as if I'm only half way through.

Yes, it's a great idea to contact as many libraries as you can, but let's be smart about this. If you're from WA, once you're already listed with suppliers like Westbooks and ALS and James Bennett, you're most of the way there.

It's still best to then contact your local library first, then go straight for the WA State Library and remind them of who you are, then try the One Library folks, then some of the bigger councils with three of four libraries in their area.

I'm gonna confess, until recently I haven't contacted a single library in WA. My books were already in some WA libraries, because the librarians have seen my books in the library supplier's lists. That's why it's so important to contact the library suppliers first, and be super professional. If the suppliers like the look of your book, they can start the selling process for you.

GET YOUR BOOK INTO AUSTRALIAN LIBRARIES

NORTHERN TERRITORY

One link for every public library in the NT, which is very handy.
   https://nt.gov.au/leisure/arts-culture-heritage/find-a-library-in-the-nt

QUEENSLAND

Type this in to your browser: http://www.slq.qld.gov.au/visit-us/find-a-public-library

In the menu bar, you'll see a button in purple with "Browse Library Services", so click that. This will open up all the main services (rather than individual library branches), so you'll only need to email the main library in each service. Explore the website and start clicking on some of the larger libraries - or any that you may have a local connection to.

NEW SOUTH WALES

Oh what a treat.
   Type this in to your browser:
   http://www.sl.nsw.gov.au/public-library-services/about-public-library-services/find-public-library-nsw

and download the Public Library Directory. 105 pages with every public library service, including addresses, librarian titles and email contacts. Again, this groups each main library service together (which can cover up to a dozen branches) and as a bonus, in many cases the main librarian's name is on the list, so you can personalise your emails to them!

ACT

All libraries in the ACT are part of ACT Government libraries. As such, there's only one email you need to send information to:
library.customerinfo@act.gov.au
I saved the easiest one for last, because I don't know about you, but I'm tired!

BONUS - NEW ZEALAND

Australians won't get lending rights from our books being in NZ's libraries, but as some of the library suppliers (Like Peter Pal and James Bennett) supply libraries there, maybe it's worth picking up new readers 'across the ditch'.
Go here
http://www.publiclibraries.org.nz/FindALibrary.aspx
With this website, click on the coloured circles, then zoom in to the 'red teardrop' on the map to get the website details of each library. Then get the email address/contact us details from each library.

OMG are you tired? I'm a wreck!

Chapter Sixteen
CONTACTING LIBRARIES

Now we're on the home stretch - it's finally time to contact the libraries themselves and show them your beautiful book.

My tip is start with your local libraries - your closest branches. This is your home base, so target them first.

You may even be on first name terms with the local librarians. (Lovely, lovely people!)

Next step, consider all the places across the state (or Australia) where you've lived or worked. Contact them, with your 'local status' claim. For example, I used to work at the Footscray Mail in my journalism days. When I contacted the City of Maribyrnong Libraries, I mentioned this.

What joy, the libraries in Maribyrnong stock all the Ondines and *1916-ish*. I told you librarians were lovely!

Now, it's possibly just a coincidence that this happened, and my titles simply appealed to their readership. Because I also previously worked at the Dandenong Journal (And I was born in the hospital there!) but so far, Dandenong and Springvale Libraries remain Ebony McKenna free. Sigh!

WHAT'S THE BEST WAY TO CONTACT LIBRARIES?

Individually.

Yep. One at a time. Check out the library service's website and see how many branches they have.

I thought I could be clever and put all my state librarian contacts into an email list and contact them all at the same time.

Guess what?

The email either went straight to their junk folder, unopened, or it was opened, but nothing happened. I know this because the book I was promoting (*The Girl and The Ghost*) has not appeared on the shelves yet. What a screaming disaster! Please learn from my mistake and go back to old fashioned one-at-a-time contacting, where you introduce yourself and your book/s and let them know they can be ordered from all the main suppliers.

SMALL PRESS AUTHORS

Your print or ebooks may already be in some libraries, so you need to know which ones are in their catalogues ahead of time. Why? Because if your earlier books are on the shelves, you'll look a bit unprofessional asking them to buy the same book again.

BUT if your earlier books are in their catalogues, it gives you a talking point for encouraging interest in the next one:

"I'm delighted my titles 'THE BEST BOOK EVER' and its sequel 'THE EVEN BETTEREST BOOK' are in your library catalogue. Now the trequel is here, 'THE EVEN BETEREST BOOKESt.'

Then let them know which suppliers stock your book, and cross your fingers that they order more in.

If the library has all your books already, then give yourself a pat on the back for writing a brilliant book that people want to read. Then move on to contacting the next library.

I'd be reluctant to put 'my books are already in 'next shire along's catalogue' in an email, in an attempt to show them you're already successful. Libraries have strict budgets, but they don't restrict borrowing privileges to people in their immediate local government area. If you specifically mention to the City of Yarra that your books are in Port Philip's libraries, (as an example) they might shrug and say, 'we'll tell our borrowers to borrow from them, if they ask for your book.' Many libraries are pooling their resources and sharing shelf space to make their budgets stretch further.

True story, my neighbour has recently acquired an ereader and he's signed up for four library services across Eastern Melbourne. He's utterly delighted because he doesn't have to drive to those libraries to borrow - just put in a request and when the book is available, it pops up on his device.

As I said in the previous chapter, my books are in some libraries across WA, but I've never approached any of them independently. The reason they're on the shelves is because the library suppliers did the work for me and promoted my books (along with thousands of others). I have since approached many, many more libraries and it's lovely to see the orders coming in.

DON'T DONATE YOUR BOOKS

This absolutely bears repeating. And I know so many of you want to take a short cut and donate your books, but please don't.

Aside from sounding like a nice idea (to you, the author), please don't donate your books to your local library - unless they've confirmed to you that they really want them.

Put it another way: If you were making clothes and all your friends loved them and said you should make more and sell them, would you take a carload to Myer and say, 'Put these on the racks?'

Probably not. You might take them to a community market,

which is completely legitimate. But if you wanted to get them on the racks at the big stores, you would most likely need to engage a supplier.

It's the same with books.

I've spoken to authors who have donated their books and the results . . . aren't that good.

One said she'd donated a paperback to her closest library and later found it on the second hand sales table. It hadn't even been catalogued.

Yes, libraries sell books. Books that don't get borrowed don't stay on the shelves for long. And, if the book was donated, it might not even be put on the shelf in the first place (which is what happened to my friend).

It might seem cruel that libraries sell books - but it's smart collections management. What's the point of keeping books on the shelves if nobody borrows them? There's only a finite amount of space, and if old books are clogging them up, there's no room for new books - books by you!

Librarian friends blanch at the thought of authors donating their books (or their entire collections.) I've heard that the State Library gets well-meaning people depositing their entire collection of "Niche Interest Monthly" dating back to the first issue in 1926. Which is impressive, but, being a State Library, they already have every issue of 'Niche Interest Monthly' and they don't need doubles.

Sometimes authors are rather insistent that their books must be donated to the library. The lovely librarian, not wanting to cause offense, accepts the books. Alas, a few weeks later, the author comes back and checks the catalogue and is upset not to see his or her books listed.

How very awkward.

Yes, I'm repeating myself because this is so important. It's why I wrote this entire book.

Having grown up with a stack of teachers and librarians in my life, I know they have an ordered way of doing things.

Libraries have long-standing collections policies, setting out how they order books and which shelving areas need replenishing and which are overstocked. Traditional publishers send out promotions about upcoming titles months in advance - so libraries can allocate their budgets.

Plus, you've read this far - either borrowing this book from a library or buying it outright - so why buy the proverbial dog if you're going to bark yourself?

Doing things the right way will help you the author, and the library, in the long run.

YOUR NEW CHECKLIST

- You've made sell sheets.
- You've made a list of libraries to contact.
- You're drafting emails ready to send (or being really brave and already sending them! Huzzah!)
- You're collapsing in a heap because this is so much work!

Time for a cup of tea (or something stronger) and a lie down.

Chapter Seventeen
BRINGING IT ALL TOGETHER

In your own time, you'll email libraries with a short but charming introduction and you'll attach your sell-sheet.

You'll give them information on how you the author can be contacted, should they have any queries.

The librarians will then decide whether your title is a good fit for their borrowers. If it's an area with an older population, then your book about later in life financial investments will be just the ticket.

If however, the library is in an area with much younger demographics who speak English as a second language, then they might pass on your investment book.

This is the 'unknown' part of the equation. Not everyone will want your book - and that's OK. What you're hoping to do is find the places where your book will be a good fit.

If the library wants your title, they will place an order with their preferred library supplier.

The supplier will either order the title directly from Ingram Spark or another printer they have a pre-existing business relationship with.

Or, the supplier will send the order directly to you, the author, to fulfil.

You need to fulfil that order in a timely fashion. So get it out that week.

Make sure you always have at least 10 copies of each of your book titles in stock. That way, if suppliers send orders directly to you, you can send copies in good time.

If you're unable to supply straight away, please let the supplier know. Sometimes there are printing issues, and there might even be a postal strike. Some things are out of your control. Simply contact them as soon as you can to let them know. Keep the communication open and professional and people will understand.

Contacting libraries was the last thing to do on the jobs list, and yet it was probably the first thing you *wanted* to do. Now that you know how 'the system' works, it will be much easier getting your next book (and the one after that) into the system, so the system starts to work for you and you start to work within the system.

Start at the beginning and work you way through.

You'll get there.

Chapter Eighteen
SCHOOL SUPPLIERS

With regards to school libraries, most will be looking to stock children's and young adult fiction. Or 'Lichery' books. (Just kidding). If your books fit in those categories, it might be worth contacting the following:

SCHOLASTIC AND OTHER TYPES OF BOOK CLUBS

These book club newsletters go out across the country, into schools (usually primary schools.) Kids (well, their parents) order discounted books, the school also gets a few books for their library and everyone is happy.

Personally, I don't see this as a guaranteed way of getting into school libraries, but every little helps, right?

My first book has appeared in these book clubs, either solo or bundled in with other similar books. Your publisher doesn't have to be Scholastic to get in, by the way (mine was Hardie Grant Egmont at the time.) But since I've gone indie, I haven't even approached them. Perhaps I should?

It's possible, if you're writing for younger readers, to get an independent book in their book club, but you'd probably have to offer it at an incredible discount. I'm not sure you'd make much of a profit, but on the other hand it could be an excellent way to reach plenty of readers.

REDGUM BOOK CLUB

NSW-based, Redgum Book Club goes out to schools offering new and discounted books and book sets, similar to Scholastic. It's well worth a google search and checking them out. They have supported indie authors in the past and I hear good things about them.

LAMONT BOOKS IN HALLAM, VICTORIA

Lamont sells directly into primary and secondary schools in Australia (mostly Victoria). They like a good 'lead time' of at least three months for a new title, in order to decide whether to stock it.

Last year I offered them *Robyn and the Hoodettes* but they turned it down because it was already released. (And there I was thinking it was new!)

But then I told them about my next book, *The Girl and The Ghost* and they were interested. They asked to read it first (yikes, I felt like I was back on submission!)

They read it.

Exactly! Lamont staff read all the books they sell, so that when they recommend books to schools, they know what they're talking about. In the end, they got back to me and said, 'yes thanks' and they placed an order for 50 books. I was pretty happy with that.

I now know how early I need to contact them for the next book, which is excellent. I love them like whoa!

The downside is they want a very deep discount on the $RRP. 65-70% usually.

ASO- AUSTRALIAN STANDING ORDERS

I contacted Belinda Bolliger from ASO - Australian Standing Orders. They supply schools with books for reading lists or for the library shelves, but a fairly narrow range of titles.

"ASO buys books from established publishers as well as self-publishers/independent authors. We buy for all age groups, from preschool through to secondary. We select titles that can generally be described as the 'literary' end of children's publishing (ie, not mass market or strongly commercial titles), the style of book that is likely to end up on the CBCA shortlist, for example.

We only buy first release titles and send them to schools in the month of their publication. We do not take backlist titles.

Quantities for young adult titles are around 900 copies. Quantities for junior fiction titles around 2,000 copies.

We buy at either 65% discount/25% returns or 70% firm sale, depending on the deal, quantities required etc.

I need to read complete, edited manuscripts approximately 4 months ahead of publication. I am currently finalising June selections and will begin on July selections next month.

Please note that there is only one of me, so it's best to send a sales information sheet before sending a manuscript for consideration. I can then let you know if I'm interested in reading the manuscript.

I'm happy to receive manuscripts by email, however if the files are very large, I suggest that you send them via wetransfer or Dropbox, or something similar.

Belinda Bolliger
Editorial Manager, **Australian Standing Orders**

Scholastic Australia Pty Ltd | PO Box 579 Lindfield, NSW, 2070 | 345 Pacific Highway, Lindfield, NSW, 2070

(02) 9413 8342 | belinda_bolliger@australianstandingorders.com.au

THE LITTLE BOOKROOM, CARLTON, VICTORIA

Leesa Lambert is the owner operator and she knows and loves books. I love going there to buy books - especially for fussy boys. (I bristle at the term 'reluctant reader'. My son will read the local newspaper, but finds a slab of small-print text really daunting. He's not reluctant, he just loves pictures in his books.) I digress.

The Little Bookroom sells to the public from their shopfront, and they sell books directly to schools via their sales reps. I have them to thank for the vast amount of the first two Ondines ending up in so many school libraries.

I'm in Victoria, and Lamont and The Little Bookroom are here in Melbourne, so it makes sense that I've contacted 'local' suppliers.

GOOGLE IS YOUR FRIEND

It's worth spending some time googling library book suppliers in your state to see what comes up closer to you. Most of them will be companies that supply chairs, tables, shelves, trolleys, stickers and labels. Everything but the books. But some actually sell books!

This link is from the PLA, Public Libraries of Australia. It's a full list of stacks of library suppliers - but not all of them supply books. However, it's a brilliant resource, so I'm sharing it here.

http://www.pla.org.au/Library_Suppliers?field_supplier_state_value=All&page=0

Chapter Nineteen
ONE MORE THING

Please visit me any time at my author website www.ebonymckenna.com and join my mailing list. By doing so, you'll get a free copy of The Summer of Shambles (Ondine 1) and other free reads along the way.

I hope you're feeling confident and filled with knowledge (so much knowledge) to get your books out there on to library shelves.

Is there anything I've missed? Please email me author@ebonymckenna.com and I'll add it to the next edition.

Come and waste some time with me on social media
facebook.com/EbonyMcKenna
twitter.com/EbonyMcKenna
www.ebonymckenna.weebly.com

Thank you, and cheers to your success.

Chapter Twenty

MARC RECORDS

Troubleshooting before you shoot me an email ...

I'm giving this subject a chapter on its own so you can find it easily. Hey, there *waves*.

This is in response to the feedback I've received since first publishing this book - which is unfailingly about MARC records not working out properly when authors register for Lending Rights.

What is a MARC record?

MARC stands for **MA**chine **R**eadable **C**ataloguing record.

If you fill in your book's details on myidentifiers.com.au (as we all need to) and then go and fill all your details into your printer/distributor such as Ingram Spark - those details need to be **exactly the same.**

I'm talking EXACT!

If you have different keywords, or a slightly different description, or different page numbers - the MARC record will not match up and you won't be able to register for Lending Rights.

It won't matter if you've sent copies off to the National Library or not (as some helpful folks at the Lending Rights department suggest).

In the 'Registering for Lending Rights' chapter in Part II, I explained it like this:

> **"Match Your Categories**
> Not only will you need to make sure the ISBN is spot on, and your titles are correctly matched; you'll need to make sure your book description is the same. Otherwise Lending Rights will have a fit and you'll get 'computer says no' treatment. Maintain consistency with correct titles, description, ISBN, publisher, keywords/categories. If there's a mismatch, Lending Rights will query your 'MARC'. MARC stands for **Ma**chine **R**eadable **C**ataloguing record."

It's easy to accidentally put the wrong information in to online forms, so I urge everyone to keep good records.

To recap:

- You will need to buy ISBNs for print editions in order to list them for Lending Rights in Australia.
- To buy ISBNs in Australia you need to purchase them through the registered retailer, Thorpe Bowker and use their myidentifiers.com.au website to list all the details of that book with the ISBN.
- Keep a record of everything you've put in myidentifiers (copy and paste into a word file if you need to) so that when you come to list your book and its ISBN and details with your printer (and with Lending Rights), you're copying and pasting the exact same information from one place to the other.

If you get rejected from Lending Rights because of the MARC record issue, then you'll need to go back through your own records and check them. Copy and paste everything from myidentifyers into a word document. Or take screen shots. Which ever way is easier for you to 'spot the difference' between different online forms.

If there's something in myidentifiers that you can't change yourself, then contact myidentifiers through the website and ask them for assistance.

Do the same for your printer/distributor (such as Blurb.com.au or Ingram Spark or Amazon etc)

Make sure every section you fill out matches the information on the other forms. Double check against the ISBN, page count, title, spelling, keywords, etc etc. Make sure everything is as exact as possible.

If there's a space that doesn't require filling (an optional field) leave it blank so there's one less thing to go wrong.

Drink all the coffee/tea/gin.

When you're absolutely certain the details in myidentifiers and your printer are identical, take those details and enter them into your Lending Rights claim(s).

As of printing, I have self-published 7 novels, 3 writing guides and a couple of anthologies. Only one novel came back with the 'MARC' situation, which I then fixed by making sure the details on myidentifiers were correct.

It can be confusing, so take it slowly.

Good luck!

ALSO BY EBONY MCKENNA

The Edit Your Own series

Edit Your Own Romance Novel

Edit Your Own YA Novel

The First 3 Chapters

The **ONDINE** series (in reading order)

The Summer of Shambles

The Autumn Palace

The Winter of Magic

The Spring Revolution

Other works:

1916-ish

Robyn and the Hoodettes

The Girl & The Ghost (2018 RWA Romantic Book of the Year)

Anthologies:

The Hauntings of Livingstone Hall

The Hauntings on the High Seas (coming soon.)

Dangerous Boys Volume 1

ACKNOWLEDGMENTS

Enormous thanks to the Romance Writers of Australia for being an incredible support network, and to the authors who signed up for this workshop in early 2018, to road-test it and prove that it works. You are awesome.

To my wonderful crit group, The Saturday Ladies' Bridge Club. We rock!

www.ingramcontent.com/pod-product-compliance
Lightning Source LLC
Chambersburg PA
CBHW072056290426
44110CB00014B/1705